Facilitating Problem-based
Learning

SRHE and Open University Press Imprint
General Editor: Heather Eggins

Facilitating Problem-based Learning

Illuminating Perspectives

Maggi Savin-Baden

The Society for Research into Higher Education
& Open University Press

Published by SRHE and
Open University Press
McGraw-Hill Education
McGraw-Hill House
Shoppenhangers Road
Maidenhead
Berkshire
England
SL6 2QL

email: enquiries@openup.co.uk
world wide web: www.openup.co.uk

and
Two Penn Plaza
New York, NY10121-2289, USA

First Published 2003
Reprinted 2007

A catalogue record of this book is available from the British Library

ISBN-10: 0 335 21054 6 (pb) 0 355 21055 4 (hb)
ISBN-13: 978 0 335 21054 1 (pb) 978 0 335 21055 8 (hb)

Library of Congress Cataloging-in-Publication Data
CIP data has been applied for

Typeset by RefineCatch Limited, Bungay, Suffolk
Printed in Great Britain by Bell and Bain, Glasgow

For my parents Frank Savin (1924–2002) and Joyce Savin, who always integrated learning with life

Contents

Acknowledgements

Thanks are due to several people who, over the last few years, have influenced and challenged my thinking and encouraged me to write. Three in particular are of note: Ron Barnett, Liz Beaty and Lewis Elton.

I would like to thank the critical friends who commented on the manuscript: Auldeen Alsop, Terry Barrett, David Boud, Barbara Duch, Lewis Elton, Della Freeth, Karen O'Rourke, James Wisdom and my mother Joyce Savin. I am also grateful to all those who have participated in my research and agreed to be quoted here. My grateful thanks are also due to Lila M. Smith for permission to use the cartoon on the front cover and to Karl A. Smith, Morse-Alumni Distinguished Professor, University of Minnesota for drawing my attention to it in the first place.

Finally, thanks are due to John Savin-Baden for his support, incisive comments, proof reading, critical sense of humour and for managing two very small children while I wrote. The views expressed here and any errors are mine.

Prologue

This book has resulted from a number of challenges and concerns that have emerged from both being a facilitator on various problem-based learning programmes and equipping other tutors to become facilitators. As a lecturer and researcher in higher education and as a consultant to those wishing to implement problem-based learning, I have developed a range of strategies, practices and perspectives about what appears to help and hinder the facilitation of problem-based learning.

When I first began using problem-based learning in 1986, it was its impact on students' learning that interested me. While I believed that learning should prompt challenge and change in students' learning and lives, there were times when I felt that problem-based learning prompted too much disjunction and challenge compared with traditional lecture-based forms of learning. It was because of this that I began exploring teachers' and students' experiences of problem-based learning. Although I knew then that facilitation was central to the process of problem-based learning, it was students' stories in which I was interested. Now, 15 years later, it is the impact of problem-based learning on staff that has inspired me to write this book. This is not only because there is relatively little to help staff to implement problem-based learning, but also because there is little support for them both personally and organizationally. Over the last 8 years I have been working with tutors, heads of department and cross-university innovators wishing to implement problem-based learning across a variety of programmes. The challenges I have experienced, in the process of 'facilitating facilitators', have echoed with many staff who have struggled to implement problem-based learning with little organizational support and ambivalent attitudes from colleagues. Having worked with such staff it became apparent that, in the context of moving towards problem-based learning, many of them were becoming increasingly confused about what it meant to be a lecturer in higher education. Initially, I believed that this related specifically to the shift in role from lecturer to facilitator, in the context of problem-based learning, but over time I began to see that it was much more complex than this. What became apparent was that staff were being expected to manage increasingly diverse and ambiguous roles.

Higher education is undergoing a massive process of change worldwide. Such change has been analysed by many in the field of higher education and political science, but the stance that has been taken has been predominantly structural in its analysis (see, for example, Scott 1995, 1998; Barnett 1997, 2000a; Coffield and Williamson 1997). Alongside such perspectives have been arguments for, and the implementation of, changes to teaching and learning in the form of the professionalization of teaching in higher education. What is missing from these analyses and arguments is a delineation of, and a practical understanding of, what it means to be a teacher in higher education and, for many, what it means to be a facilitator in problem-based learning.

Thus the agenda for writing this book stemmed from a fascination about the ways in which staff were and were not managing themselves and their roles in the context of problem-based learning. It also emerged from concerns I had about the ways in which the implementation of problem-based learning was, and was not, being facilitated in the wider sphere of the organization and of higher education in general. The somewhat ambiguous title of this book allows for a consideration of a broad range of issues about facilitation, in particular:

- understandings of facilitation;
- staff expectations and experiences of facilitation;
- the implementation of problem-based learning curricula;
- equipping and supporting staff;
- exploring the impact of adopting problem-based learning wholesale as a university learning strategy.

Problem-based learning revisited

Problem-based learning continues to be used in diverse ways across different subjects and disciplines worldwide. Yet there remains confusion about the difference between problem-based learning and problem-solving learning. To summarize: in problem-solving learning, the learning problem scenarios are set within and are bounded by a discrete subject or disciplinary area. In some curricula, students are given specific training in problem-solving techniques, but in many cases they are not. The focus in this kind of learning is largely upon acquiring the answers expected by the lecturer, answers that are rooted in the information supplied in some way to the students. Thus the solutions are always linked to a specific curricular content which is seen as vital for students to cover for them to be competent and effective practitioners. In problem-based learning, the focus is on organizing the curricular content around problem scenarios rather than subjects or disciplines. Students work in groups or teams to resolve or manage these scenarios but they are not expected to acquire a predetermined series of right answers. Instead, they are expected to engage with the complex scenario presented to them and decide what information they need to learn and what skills they need to gain in order to manage the situation effectively.

Problem-based learning is increasingly being seen as a means of educating students to learn with complexity. What I mean is that problem-based learning helps students to see that learning and life take place in contexts, contexts that affect the kinds of solutions that are available and possible. Yet it would also appear to be a form of learning that is seen as a means of equipping them for what Barnett (2000a) has termed 'supercomplexity', the idea that the frameworks by which we understand the world are multiplying and thus professional life is increasingly characterized by the need to manage multiple frameworks of understanding, action and self-identity. The consequence, Barnett has argued, is that teaching 'has to be construed as the production of supercomplexity in the private space of the minds of students' (Barnett 2000a: 162). However, what is missing from this argument is the means by which it is possible to help students to become the kinds of beings who can function in the kind of world that Barnett has delineated. Helping students to become equipped for such a world is surely the role of the lecturer in higher education. Yet it would appear that what it means to be a lecturer is contestable. How many of us now actually lecture? If we do, what is our purpose in doing so? It would appear that being a lecturer in higher education is becoming an increasingly complex task. This is not just because we have to be multi-skilled, multi-task beings who lecture, research, administrate, budget, publish and consult, to name but a few, but because the nature of what it means to be a teacher in higher education is changing. The shifts towards a culture of improving teaching through forms of training, which focus on behavioural rather than personal and attitudinal change, are at odds for many of us with our beliefs that learning to facilitate is a complex and multifaceted capability. Facilitation invariably demands that we make personal shifts away from long-held beliefs about the nature of knowledge and notions of learning.

In many universities, the adoption of problem-based learning is adding another dimension to what it means to be a lecturer in higher education. Many staff feel that when implementing problem-based learning they have an intuitive understanding of what it means to be a facilitator. Some of us may be able to articulate what it means, but few of us have ever really explored the relationship between our different notions of teaching in higher education, or been able to take the risk to share such personally challenging perspectives in a public forum. To do so would be to invite criticism of the role confusions and conflicts that many of us feel, as the boundaries of our jobs change and move, with the shifts in the organizational cultures that we experience daily. Yet there is not only little help available for those wishing to become facilitators of problem-based learning and for the challenges that utilizing such an approach demands of lecturers, but also little real acknowledgement of the impact of the current global shift towards problem-based learning. To suggest that there is a global shift might seem a little overstated, yet there does appear to be such a shift, as universities in Europe and South Africa, Hong Kong, Singapore and the USA seek to turn swathes of curricula problem-based.

The argument

My argument centres around one main theme and five sub-themes that I will discuss throughout the book. The main argument is that the notion of facilitation in problem-based learning is too narrow. There needs to be a wider conception of facilitation whereby the acadame understand that problem-based learning is not necessarily a safe pedagogic option. It needs to be acknowledged that facilitation is not just about staff helping students to learn in small groups. What is needed instead is that the academe takes on, rather than falls short of, its responsibility towards the academic community and the marketplace.

Narrow conceptualizations of facilitation have, to date, meant that issues connected with a wider view of facilitation have been left uncontested. This has resulted in the following:

1. There is little support at an organizational level for staff who are problem-based learning facilitators. There appears to be an assumption by lecturing staff that the university supports the implementation of problem-based learning if the leadership supports it verbally, at say a university-wide staff development day, and thereafter does not interfere too much in what staff are doing. The result is that few staff receive adequate staff development to equip them to be a facilitator or sufficient time to develop materials. University leaders who argue for the adoption of problem-based learning within their universities must be prepared to support such a development by providing realistic funding and preparation time.

2. Not enough attention is being paid to the role of the facilitator in problem-based learning. There is little understanding of, or research into, the complex interplay between team and facilitator and the ways in which they both change and adapt their roles and relationships as the problem-based learning team matures.

3. There is little understanding of the impact of the facilitator on students' learning in problem-based learning teams. For example, there has been an underestimation of the impact of individual staff members' personal stances and motivations as a teacher on their ability to facilitate problem-based learning. There is an assumption that all staff can facilitate a problem-based learning team effectively, whereas the strengths of some may lie elsewhere, such as being an excellent lecturer. This has resulted in a lack of understanding about what it means to facilitate problem-based learning in ways that promote learning for all students.

4. Issues of assessment continue to be under debate in problem-based learning. There needs to be not only a delineation of the issues for students in relation to assessment, but also an understanding of the role of the facilitator in the assessment process.

5. Much is claimed for problem-based learning, particularly in terms of the promotion of key skills and effective teamwork. Although there is some evidence to support many of the claims, there needs to be an examination of how staff help students develop honesty in teams and discourage unethical practices.

While this whole argument would seem very negative, the criticism is not laid at the door of the many staff who have battled to promote and implement problem-based learning in ways that exemplify sound teaching practices. Rather, it is designed to point out that if problem-based learning continues to be adopted as a major component of university teaching and learning strategies, it would be wise to engage with these issues so as to avoid expensive mistakes.

The plan

Part 1 explores the current position of problem-based learning from a global perspective. Chapter 1 begins by investigating the current research and literature on problem-based learning and facilitation in general, argues that the problem-based community is a rhetorical one and then compares problem-based learning with other similar approaches such as work-based learning and action learning. Chapter 2 takes a critical look at what it means to facilitate learning in problem-based contexts and explores issues of responsibility, ownership and accountability for staff and students. In particular, it examines the notion of types of, or approaches to, facilitation and presents and critiques some of the current models on offer. These chapters provide the platform for the development of the central argument that the notion of facilitation is currently too narrowly construed in the world of higher education.

Part 2 explores notions of problem-based learning and facilitation from teachers' and students' perspectives. This section is based on several different studies that have been undertaken to illuminate staff perspectives when facilitating problem-based learning. This section also draws on earlier research examining the impact of teachers' interactional stances on students' learning. Chapter 3 demonstrates the transitions staff have made personally and pedagogically when moving from the role of lecturer to that of facilitator. In particular, it examines the evolving role of problem-based learning tutors in terms of their adaptation to the team over time and in relation to the increasing sophistication of the learners. It explores how different facilitators have dealt with dysfunctional teams and examines the strategies facilitators have used to deal with students' concerns about the quality of their learning. Chapter 4 examines the notion of effective facilitation; in particular, it explores the idea of what counts as being effective at different levels and in diverse contexts. This chapter also explores various processes that facilitators use to prepare students for problem-based learning and the ways they help them to adapt to it as an approach to learning. It suggests ways of ensuring equity of participation by students in the team and mechanisms to equip students in the development of critical thought. The final chapter in this section, Chapter 5, explores the underlying assumptions about students' views of learning through problem-based learning and examines the notions of ethics and honesty when working in learning teams.

Part 3 explores the notion of facilitation by exploring particular areas, such as staff development, honesty and assessment, which have an impact on the implementation of problem-based learning. Chapter 6 suggests ways of providing staff development in relation to problem-based learning. Suggestions are made about ways of executing staff development programmes and providing mechanisms for continuing support for staff as they implement problem-based learning. Chapter 7 examines current notions of facilitation in relation to virtual environments and new forms of learning communities. It examines current and emerging trends in the use of computer-mediated and multi-media problem-based learning. Chapter 8 concludes this section by unpacking the relationship between assessment and facilitation. I argue that although assessment has been discussed widely in relation to problem-based learning, few of the difficulties have been resolved and that relatively little has been discussed about the role of the facilitator in relation to team, peer and self-assessment.

The final chapters of the book explore the issues of facilitation in relation to the changing world of higher education. Chapter 9 examines what is meant by curriculum and in particular the shifts that have taken place towards more mechanistic formulations of curricula than in former years. It considers the way in which change towards more authoritarian forms of leadership in universities has affected the extent to which it is possible to implement problem-based learning curricula that enable students to develop independence in inquiry. Chapter 10 surveys the impact of implementing wide-scale problem-based learning on the higher education sector and examines what it means to implement and facilitate different kinds of problem-based learning curricula in different kinds of institutional settings. In particular, it analyses types of curriculum models that help and hinder learning in problem-based curricula. The epilogue reflects on the consequences of our current global position and suggests ways that we can begin to effect change.

Part 1

Re-viewing Facilitation

1

Perspectives on Facilitation

Introduction

'So what exactly is facilitation in problem-based learning?' my colleague asked, one Friday evening after work, while relaxing in a rooftop bar. As I struggled to explain that facilitation wasn't just about sitting with a group of students while they got on with the learning and that it also wasn't some form of psychodynamic group counselling, it occurred to me that explaining problem-based learning facilitation oppositionally might possibly be a good starting point. As I drove home I began to wonder if facilitation had been defined too narrowly, or whether in fact notions about what counted as good facilitation were largely related to the extent to which a tutor helped students to meet the learning outcomes from the problem scenario. These reflections marked the unpacking of many of the complexities involved in facilitating problem-based learning that I had thought about for over a year, but not really engaged with in any depth. Thus in this book I argue that current understandings and definitions of problem-based learning facilitation are too narrow and that we need to re-examine and redefine them.

This chapter begins by arguing that the problem-based learning community has particular characteristics and that this has several implications for higher education. It goes on to explore the problem-based community, analyses some of the reasons why problem-based learning facilitation is construed too narrowly, and examines how this might be contested to promote a wider conception of facilitation. It then sets problem-based learning in context by exploring the relationship between problem-based learning and other similar approaches, such as work-based learning and simulations.

A problem-based curriculum or a problem-based community?

As noted earlier, there is continuing debate about what counts as problem-based learning and what does not, at both local and global levels. What is perhaps more important than defining bounded parameters for problem-based learning is to explore instead the community of problem-based learning and what this tells us. There are now many global consultants, keynote speakers, books, journals, magazines and websites related to the subject of problem-based learning. Looking at each of these, there are differences between them in the particular stance they take, but broadly speaking one sees more similarities than differences. There is thus a sense that the problem-based learning community is a rhetorical one. What I mean by this is that members of such a community have shared parameters about what counts as evidence and ways of refuting an argument because they share a rhetorical vision. They have a desire to belong to the same club because they share common ground. It is a community with a shared vision, a shared language that comprises codes and slogans, and several ideological and procedural assumptions.

I have previously written about the untold stories of staff and students in a variety of contexts in an attempt to capture the idea that there are still many gaps in our understandings of staff and students' experiences of problem-based learning. There still remain many untold stories in the community, but in this chapter the notion of the problem-based learning community as a rhetorical community will be explored to examine some of its complex and symbolic features. Rhetorical criticism is concerned with the analysis and interpretations of meanings expressed in rhetorical artifacts (Foss 1989) and these will be explored later in the chapter. I first consider the perspectives of several academics new to problem-based learning, which will help set some of the issues in context.

Several years ago I was running a series of overseas workshops on problem-based learning. Having set up my argument for problem-based learning, we began to debate the possibilities for implementing problem-based learning in curricula. Many of the staff had read extensively about problem-based learning before my arrival. Each member of the workshop had assumed that everyone else under-stood problem-based learning as a concept and approach, and knew the impact it would have on staff teaching and student experience when the curriculum was adapted to problem-based learning. Yet when the discussion began about ways of changing the curriculum to support problem-based learning, there was silence and disjunction. Staff had read the theory but not understood the reality. Similarly, when speaking to an environmental scientist at a different university, we were clearly at cross-purposes. He described an innovative learning experience he had set up for students that mirrored real life in vital and interesting ways. I was impressed, but as we talked it dawned on me that despite the speech I had just given and the ensuing debate, he had missed the point. He had assumed that both projects and simulations were the same as problem-based learning. While it could be said that all these learning strategies contain elements that demand the ability to solve problems, there are fundamental differences between them and problem-based learning.

Rival or rhetorical pedagogies?

There has been much discussion about the implementation of problem-based learning and the possibilities for its execution (e.g. Boud and Feletti 1997; Glen and

Wilkie 2000; Duch *et al.* 2001). There are those who would prefer that problem-based learning is upheld as an approach that works best when implemented wholesale across the curriculum, whereas others believe the issues relating to problem-based learning and curriculum design relate less to the positioning and adoption of it across a whole curriculum and more to the quality of curriculum design, however large or small that component happens to be. These are not rival pedagogies but instead rhetorical ones. What I mean is that although it may seem from texts and speeches that there is an evangelistic strand to the problem-based learning community that seeks to convert the souls who are perceived to belong to the wider, more liberal end of the church, there is little real rivalry across the spectrum. What is at play instead is essentially a diversity in rhetoric rather than a fracture in the pedagogy. The idea of explaining the problem-based community from the stance of rhetorical criticism offers an opportunity to explore both the medium and the message of the approach. The interpretation of meaning within the problem-based learning community can help us to understand the way in which dramatic narratives are projected and help us to see the characters, plots and storylines that are at play globally. Those wanting to implement problem-based learning tend to call in a consultant or attend a workshop to help them to decode the coded messages of the problem-based learning literature. Thus we can already begin to see the hallmarks of a rhetorical community emerging. These hallmarks become apparent if fantasy theme analysis is used to examine them. This approach allows an exploration of the views of rhetorical communities by revealing what the participants of such a community experience, feel, share and write about in relation to the community and the visions of the community. Thus the kinds of hallmarks we see in the problem-based learning community are:

1. Ideological and procedural assumptions, including:
   - problem-based learning will be carried out in particular ways;
   - it is an effective method of learning;
   - through problem-based learning students will become independent inquirers;
   - problem-based learning for 'critical contestability' (Savin-Baden 2000a) is a model to strive for;
   - certain plots and storylines are more acceptable than others.

2. There are codes, slogans and keywords that are accepted by the community. These are understood by those in the community and promulgated by those in leading roles, such as consultants in problem-based learning, authors of texts and keynote speakers, who tame and structure the messiness of problem-based learning through the use of these codes.

3. An affective domain emerges out of the collective excitement of the group. Foss (1989) has illustrated how such symbolic convergence might emerge:

   > A group member, for example, may tell a story in which the characters enact a particular dramatic scenario. One or more of the others will be caught up in the narrative and begin to add to it. In such instances, a number of people become deeply involved in the discussion, excitedly adding their input and playing with ideas and themes. The members'

participation in a fantasy also may be communicated non-verbally. Facial expression, bodily posture, and sounds such as laughter and moaning all indicate such participation

(Foss 1989: 120)

This could be describing a coffee break discussion at a national study day on problem-based learning, a discussion at a conference dinner or a component of a three-day workshop in problem-based learning for experienced facilitators. Symbolic convergence theory can help us to unpack this further by using it to examine the way in which symbols or symbolic terminology is used.

Through the consistent use of symbols, forms of communication are created that are particular to the problem-based learning community. Symbolic convergence theory is based on the belief that communication creates reality. For example, in group interaction, people try to make sense of what is occurring and they do this by using symbols to frame their understanding. In this case, the symbols might be models of problem-based learning (e.g. Savin-Baden 2000a) or particular symbolic terminology that helps them describe what is occurring. Communication creates reality by helping people to make sense through the use of shared symbols. This theory was developed by Bormann (1972) from Bales' (1970) studies of small group dynamics. Bales noted that, within group interaction, difficult tasks often prompted some members to experience anxiety so that, during moments of stress, group members would release tension by becoming dramatic and telling stories. Take, for example, a time in a problem-based learning session when the students have been presented with a problem scenario with which few are familiar. One member of the team may be worried about a practical assessment the next day. She believes that problem-based learning promotes self-direction, but a practical examination at which she is expected to memorize the right answers in order to perform is at odds with problem-based learning. Thus she says to the rest of the team, 'This is like a game with changing rules and we don't even know if we are playing chess or charades'. The team can choose to accept this fantasy and elaborate on it or do nothing. If the team chooses to engage with this thought and expand upon it, a chain reaction takes place. This process of dramatizing relies upon unrelated thoughts or ideas and Bales (1950, 1970) labelled these 'fantasy'. The idea of fantasy is not an illusory statement but instead is one that has little to do with the current task and through dramatizing spreads to others within the group when:

- elements are selected for more extended group discussion,
- accidents are taken advantage of for the creation of symbolic meaning,
- the selected elements and chance combinations are elaborated,
- the elaboration is performed as a cooperative process, and
- the group process has the qualities of a chain reaction – a process that reinforces itself increasingly in an accelerated growth curve of interest, excitement, and involvement.

(Bales 1950: 150)

If we take this a step further, we can see the fantasy theme method played out in the practices of problem-based learning, whereby groups of people manufacture and project dramatic narratives; in the case of problem-based learning, this could be texts, websites and conferences. Thus narratives are played out in the setting up and enacting of problem-based learning – the texts and websites offer scripts on how to handle the plots, characters and scenes connected with problem-based learning. However, one difficulty that has come to the fore in recent years is that few scripts on problem-based learning go beyond the first act of the play – we know the opening lines and the beginning of the plot, but few texts and studies can help us to see and understand how the whole curriculum might be played out. It is as if at the moment we have many one-act plays but few complete dramas. The problem-based learning community is in the process of realizing that the later acts are missing and so it is now creating spaces in which to share storylines and experts to help them to write the next scenes. So there is a growth in problem-based learning conferences and in the desire to use consultants to help implementation. This convergence has thus resulted in a community that has tribal features but, unlike the features argued for in disciplinary tribes, this tribe tends to have a foot in both camps. In terms of identity, staff will describe themselves in terms of their involvement with a discipline, and their membership of the tribe is presented through symbols such as idols: 'The culture of the discipline includes idols: the pictures on the walls and dust jackets of books kept in view are of Albert Einstein and Max Planck and Robert Oppenheimer in the office of the physicist and of Max Weber and Karl Marx and Emile Durkheim in the office of the sociologist' (Clark 1980: 4). Yet there are different members of this tribe. There are those who undertake problem-based learning, purely within their discipline and so maintain the boundaries, traditions and culture of that discipline. There are those who sit at the borders of their own discipline with a more generic view. For instance, they may be involved in teaching sociology as a component of a degree in medicine and by being involved in problem scenarios that largely centre on sociological concerns, but they are anxious to ensure that there is some integration between their discipline and the profession in which it is being taught. Finally, there are members of the tribe who have, as it were, gone native and see the value of having a disciplinary base to give them an academic home if required but who transcend the boundaries of their discipline, work in and across other disciplines and are happy to facilitate problem-based learning teams who are engaging with a problem scenario that only has loose links with their field of expertise. Thus what we are beginning to see globally is the development and emergence of a rhetorical vision. Foss stated:

> The presence of a rhetorical vision suggests that a rhetorical community has been formed consisting of participants in the vision or members who have shared the fantasy themes. The people who participate in a rhetorical vision, then, constitute a rhetorical community. They share common symbolic ground and respond to messages in ways that are in tune with their rhetorical vision: 'They will cheer references to the heroic persona in their rhetorical vision. They will respond with antipathy to allusions of the villains. They will have agreed-upon procedures for problem solving communication. They will share the same vision of what counts as evidence, how to build a case and how to refute an argument'.
>
> (Foss 1989: 125–6)

Much of this resonates with the process, messages, guidelines and principles put out by the problem-based learning community. However, the impact of this needs to be examined through an exploration of the underlying purposes of facilitation.

What is interesting about many of the arguments about whether something counts as being problem-based learning or not is the position of the teacher within the learning process. Although much has been written about teacher approaches and facilitator styles, few have explored the impact of teachers' approaches on students' learning in the problem-based context. The result has been not only a confusion about what counts as facilitation, but also a recognition of the subtle difference between facilitation in other forms of action-orientated learning, such as work-based learning and project-based learning – but we will come to these later. First, it is important to examine some of the recent studies of facilitation in problem-based learning. Although much has been documented about the role of the facilitator in small-group teaching (Rogers 1983; Heron 1989; Jaques 2000), there have been few studies in the field of problem-based learning, although there has been considerable philosophizing. For example, Margetson (1993) offered an in-depth consideration of the relationship between teaching and facilitation. He argued that extreme interpretations of facilitation, which he termed 'Content Free' (CF-facilitation), cast the facilitator in the role of midwife. Such facilitators assist in the birth of feelings and thoughts students may have, and are prohibited from influencing the content of what is produced. Facilitation such as this is seen, there-fore, as a technical function that focuses purely on process and ignores content. Margetson has claimed that what is required is a notion of teaching and learning that is 'educative' and which avoids the extremes of content-only and process-only practice:

> Educative teaching *practices* a process-content whole which cannot be exclusively separated out into a component of process and a component of content. It is *facilitative* in encouraging the learner's active, co-operative participation in extending, enriching, and transforming what is most valuable in existing meaningfulness – that is, it facilitates the learner's extension of his or her own understanding and knowledge *in relation to* the knowledge and understanding of others both current and past.
>
> (Margetson 1993: 168)

Despite this sound argument, Margetson has not explored the complexities of diverse facilitator roles and styles within teams at differing stages of team develop-ment. Facilitator roles and styles can and do affect the kind of educative teaching on offer. The symbolic use of the midwife would also seem to convey a misconstru-ing of the complexities of the role of this particular health professional, who may not influence what is produced but who may inform or guide *how* it is produced.

The learning context also needs to be taken into account when considering team change and development and the role of the facilitator within that. It is often assumed that a learning context is something that can be defined according to the situation and perhaps even the disciplinary area of study. Yet learning con-texts are transient in nature and much of the real learning that takes place for students occurs beyond the parameters of presented material but with and through others – that is, learning in relation. Since educational programmes are temporary environments, it is important to raise students' awareness of the changing nature of the learning environment, peers and tutors, and themselves within it. Therefore, recognition of the relationship between staff's espoused theories and theories-in-use, in conjunction with students' perceptions of the formal learning context, is key to facilitating students' ability to manage team learning effectively.

In terms of research into facilitation in problem-based learning, Gijselaers and Schmidt (1990) found that tutor action had a direct causal influence on small-group tutorials, which, in turn, influenced students' interest in the subject matter. These findings reflect the complexities involved in the facilitation of problem-based learning. Dolmans *et al.* (1994a) developed an instrument to assess tutor performance in problem-based learning tutorial groups, but the scales made no allowance for the inclusion of personal attributes as suggested by Heron (1989) and Jaques (2000). The tutor evaluation questionnaire comprised 13 statements concerning the tutors' behaviour. Although this instrument was found to be valid and reliable, it did not account for changes in group process or the need for different types of facilitation at different stages in the programme. A further shortcoming of this study was the lack of definition of what constituted an effective facilitator role. In a second study, Dolmans and co-workers (1994b) argued that tutor evaluation should be embedded in a broader faculty development programme. This should include the development of the formal role of the tutor, the stimulation of faculty dialogue, the design of a tutor reward system and remedial learning opportunities for tutors. They concluded that when effort is devoted to a tutor development programme, increased attention is paid by teaching tutors to teaching activities within the medical school.

More recently, research has concentrated on perceptions of group dynamics (Mpofu *et al.* 1998), the role of the facilitator (Neville 1999) and the perceived effectiveness of tutors. Extensive and leading quantitative research in this area has been undertaken at the University of Maastricht for several years. Recent work (De Grave *et al.* 1998, 1999) has focused on developing and testing a tutor intervention profile to determine the profiles of effective and less effective tutors. De Grave *et al.* suggested that the profile distinguishes between tutors who focus students upon the acquisition of propositional knowledge ('expert knowledge') and those who use process skills to stimulate learning. Their findings indicate that tutors who stress learning process rather than content acquisition are perceived to be more effective – although, as they point out, the differences were not statistically significant. What is problematic about many of these studies is that they tend to generalize the behaviour and outcomes of facilitators, rather than explore the impact of tutors' particular personal and pedagogical stances in the nature and process of facilitation. Furthermore, the notion of learning context and the impact of that context on student learning are rarely seen as variables that needs to be accounted for.

There has been much discussion about whether tutors need to be content experts when facilitating problem-based learning. In a recent study, Kaufman and Holmes (1998) reported that content experts found it more difficult to maintain a facilitator role than those who were not. Yet Neville (1999), in a review of the role of the tutor in problem-based learning, suggested that novice students with little experience of such learning would probably benefit from directive tutors who were knowledge experts. He argued that such tutors would help students to construct a foundation on which to build their learning. He suggested that students experienced in problem-based learning required less direction as they became increasingly self-sufficient. What is important about Neville's examination of the issues relating to problem-based facilitation is his acknowledgement that different situations require different tutor behaviour to facilitate student learning, findings supported by a recent study by Wilkie (2002) that will be presented in Chapter 4.

Situating problem-based learning

One difficulty in enabling people to understand the difference between problem-based learning and other similar approaches to learning relates to comprehension of curriculum design. The design of the curriculum is central to effecting problem-based learning because of the way in which the design impinges upon teachers' and students' roles and responsibilities, and the ways in which learning and knowledge are perceived. It is possible, in many conventional curricula, to add on project-based learning, games and simulations and work-based learning in a variety of ways. However, bolting on problem-based learning is usually quite difficult because of the need for inquiry and student-centred practices to be central to the learning approach. Problem-based curricula should ideally be designed with the problem scenarios as the central component of each module, so that lectures, seminars and skill laboratories can feed into them so as to inform students, rather than offering them great chunks of propositional knowledge that they may find difficult to integrate into their understanding. Designing a curriculum based on content and disciplinary knowledge and then trying to make it problem-based usually ends in disaster. So whether it is a module or an entire programme that is designed to be problem-based, the starting point should be a set of problem scenarios that will equip students to become independent inquirers, who see learning and epistemology as flexible entities and perceive that there are other valid ways of seeing things besides their own perspective. Thus to argue that facilitation in problem-based learning differs from other teaching methods, I will begin by delineating the differences between problem-based learning and some similar approaches and techniques. Some of these, such as project-based learning, have been used extensively for many years, whereas others, such as work-based learning, are relatively recent developments. New forms of problem-based learning have also emerged, in particular computer-mediated problem-based learning and media-led problem-based learning, which will be discussed in depth in Chapter 7.

Work-based learning

Work-based learning is used here to describe learning through work so that learning occurs through engaging in a work role. The formulation of partnership is seen to have a central place in the discourses of work-based learning, and partnership as a concept operates in a variety of ways. First, the funders of work-based learning are 'in partnership' with higher education institutions. Under this arrangement, institutions such as universities largely relinquish their right to design and implement any curriculum during work-based periods. The second form of partnership is that between university and learner. Here the concept of partnership in the work-based learning debate is more problematic than the first example cited, because the higher education institutions see the individual as learner rather than employee. The focus on learner-managed learning promoted by the higher education institution is problematic not just because of issues of direction and autonomy, but because the individual is left to manage the complexity of being perceived by the university as a learner and by the employer as an employee. Yet at the same time, the learner remains the main stakeholder in a tripartite partnership between university, employee and individual.

Work-based learning is an important development in many professions but one of the key shifts it has prompted is a move away from higher education as front end education that equips people for work. Instead, initiatives such as work-based learning have promoted on-going learning, regular updating and continuing professional development, which in many ways have meant that higher education institutions have had to become more responsive to the needs of the learner. Work-based learning is not usually perceived as a problem-based approach to learning because it centres on learning through work and tends to be individually guided and focused on solving problems in the immediate work environment. The difference between work-based learning and problem-based learning is that in work-based learning the learning is derived from utilizing opportunities, resources and experience in the workplace and, therefore, the outcomes will relate to the purposes of the workplace. Work-based learning is perceived to be located at the workplace with support from the employer and university. Problem-based learning most often takes place as a component of a higher education qualification where curricula organization occurs around problems rather than disciplines, is usually undertaken in collaborative teams and where students are expected to develop capabilities for the workplace and the ability to be life-long learners.

Project-based learning

Project-based learning is seen by many to be synonymous with problem-based learning because they are both perceived to be student-centred approaches to learning. Indeed, some have argued that they are the same (Boud 1985). There are others who believe that problem-based learning can only be undertaken in small groups (Barrows and Tamblyn 1980), whereas many believe that project-based learning can be undertaken individually, as well as in small groups. Arguably, research projects, particularly doctoral dissertations, could be said to be the ultimate problem-based approach. However, I suggest that there are distinct differences between the two approaches and that these are most marked when considering curriculum design, rather than in terms of one approach necessarily being more effective than the other.

Project-based learning is predominately task-orientated and the project is often set by the tutor. Even if the task or topic is not set, then the parameters and criteria for submission usually are. The differences between the two approaches are as follows:

- In project-based learning, students are required to produce an outcome in the form of a report or design, whereas in problem-based learning, the focus is not on this kind of outcome.
- In project-based learning, the tutor supervises (rather than facilitates) the project.
- In project-based learning, students are required to produce a solution or strategy to *solve* the problem, whereas in problem-based learning, solving the problem may be part of the process but the focus is on problem management, not on a clear and bounded solution.
- An input from the tutor occurs in project-based learning, in the form of some type of teaching, during the lifespan of the project. The focus in problem-based learning is on students working out their own learning requirements. Some problem-based learning programmes use lectures as a means to support the students rather than to direct the learning.
- In project-based learning, students are usually involved in the choice of project (sometimes from a predetermined list). In problem-based learning, students may choose problem scenarios from practice although the problems are usually provided by staff, but what and how they learn is defined by the students.
- Project-based learning often occurs towards the end of a degree programme after a given body of knowledge has been covered that will equip the students to undertake the project. Problem-based learning is not usually used on the basis that students have already covered required propositional knowledge; rather, students themselves are expected to decide what it is they need to learn.
- In project-based learning, the project group/team only come together for the duration of the project. In problem-based learning, the students are put into learning teams* for a large component of the course. This means they have to learn to work together as a team and overcome the challenges of being part of a committed learning team and not a short-term project team.
- Project-based learning is often seen as a mechanism for bringing together several subject areas under one overall activity at the end of a course. Problem-based learning works from the premise that learning necessarily will occur across disciplinary boundaries, even at the beginning of a course.

---

* The word 'team' is used throughout the book to denote a group of people who work together with a common purpose, with a limited membership and the power to make decisions. Teams have a focus, a set of team rules and are time-limited. The term team is more appropriate for what occurs in most problem-based learning seminars because there is a focus, a remit and much of the learning that occurs evolves through the ways in which the team makes decisions about what and how they learn within agreed or contracted deadlines.

Project-based learning, therefore, is more often seen as a teaching technique in a given area of the curriculum rather than an overall educational strategy such as problem-based learning.

Action learning

Action learning is based on the idea that through the process of reflection and action, it is possible to solve problems. The idea is that a group of people come together to form an action learning set. The set work together over a stated period of time with the aim of 'getting things done' (McGill and Beaty 2001: 1). In practice, this means that the set is formed and each member brings a real-life problem they want help to solve. Action learning is a form of learning based on the interrelationship of learning and action and thus the learning occurs through a continuous process of reflecting and acting by the individual on their problem.

The learning set is designed to be more than a straightforward support group, because the role of set members is to help individual members to deal with their particular problem. However, a set is not a formal meeting with an agenda, nor is it a counselling group or a critical incident analysis in the staff room over lunch. Instead, it is a formalized process whereby the set meet on a regular basis to undertake action that will deal with or resolve problems and thus the focus of the set is on the learning from the actions taken by the individual. The set lifespan tends to vary between 6 months and 3 years.

The difference between problem-based learning and action learning is that the essence of an action learning set is its focus on the individual and their future action (McGill and Beaty 2001: 14–15). In problem-based learning, the group functions as a team whick seeks to achieve the tasks collaboratively, the lifespan is generally determined by the length of the module or curriculum and there is usually a facilitator who is a member of staff. Thus in action learning the members have more control over the set than many students would do in a problem-based learning team, where the facilitator may influence the learning agenda and in some curricula the problem-based session may appear to contain components of a seminar where presentations are made and pre-prepared material is discussed. Action learning sets are more individualized, freer flowing and centred upon personal learning and reflection to achieve effective action.

Games and simulations

Games are usually described as exercises in which individuals cooperate or compete within a given set of rules (Jaques 2000), such as charades, tiddlywinks or hockey; thus players act as themselves. Simulations are when a scenario is provided that in some way represents real life. The confusions that occur between problem-based learning and simulations relate to the use of real-life situations. In problem-based learning, students are (usually) provided with real-life scenarios, they are expected to act as themselves and the situations with which they are presented are tailored according to the level of the course. In simulations, individuals are ascribed roles related to the simulations, such as 'you are the manager of an engineering firm' or 'your aim in this simulation is to win the most money', with the tutor acting as a referee.

Games and simulations can increase students' motivation for learning and facilitate team building. They are useful in the initial stages of problem-based learning to develop the team and they can also be used in conjunction with a real-life problem-based learning scenario. However, if the simulation or game is not linked to other knowledge and capabilities within the curriculum, then learning may be perceived as time-consuming and superficial. Thus debriefing is vital in these approaches to promote effective engagement and learning (see, for example, Pearson and Smith 1985).

Conclusion

Since its inception in medical schools in the 1960s, interest has grown in problem-based learning and such growth can be seen in the number of curricula and modules that now adopt it as their guiding principle. The surge in interest is perhaps due to the promise that it seems to hold for helping us to achieve our multiple and often divergent educational goals. However, the approach is not without challenges, not least because of the confusion about its relationship with other forms of action-orientated learning. This chapter has presented an overview of some of the developing issues connected with facilitating problem-based learning, such as the growth of a problem-based community and the challenges that arise when trying to delineate differences between other learning approaches that have similar aims and characteristics as problem-based learning, but which are often used for different motives. The next chapter examines types and approaches to facilitation and critiques some of the current models on offer.

2

Types and Levels of Facilitation

Introduction

The concept of facilitation was dealt with in Chapter 1 predominantly in terms of a discussion of the literature and the research that has been undertaken. However, when the topic of facilitation is being discussed at conferences and in workshops, many people appear to be interested in what counts as facilitation, the way that it differs from other forms of teaching, what it means to be an effective facilitator and how facilitation affects students and their learning. Broadly speaking, facilitation can be considered at a number of levels and such levels will be explored throughout the book, but an overview is offered here first. The main thrust of this chapter will be an exploration of how facilitation is conceptualized and practised. Becoming a facilitator and being an effective facilitator will be dealt with later in Part Two, in Chapters 4 and 5. In this chapter, facilitation will be explored from the perspective of what it is that is being facilitated and how facilitation is conceptualized. Although several facilitation models exist (e.g. Rogers 1983; Heron 1989), it will be argued that facilitation is context-bound. Universal models of facilitation may be informative but it is not possible to use them as templates to ensure that every facilitator in each curriculum context is facilitating the problem-based learning team in the same way at the same level of the programme. Instead, I argue that facilitation is related to teachers' and students' 'learner stances', in particular their pedagogical stances (Savin-Baden 2000a), and that patterns or approaches will emerge but may change over time.

Facilitating learning?

Too few debates have taken place about the nature and process of facilitation in problem-based learning. Although the research and literature on these topics is growing (as we have seen in Chapter 1), there has been relatively little discussion about what is being facilitated – students' understanding and enactment of problem-based learning, the team process, the process of learning, individual learning, the achievement of the learning outcomes or the tutor's ability to facilitate? If we first examine the overall purposes of implementing problem-based learning that are adhered to by many, we can then set this up against some of the issues for staff, students and institutions implementing problem-based learning.

Facilitating student learning

The arguments that problem-based learning improves student learning in a variety of different ways continue. Although the arguments are often persuasive, the literature used to support such claims is increasingly under debate. For example, many authors continue to suggest that problem-based learning promotes deep approaches (as opposed to surface or strategic approaches) to learning, the under-lying assumption being that this is necessarily a good thing. The concept of surface approaches to learning emerged from the work of Marton and Säljö (1984), who distinguished two different approaches to learning: learners who could concentrate on memorizing what the author wrote (surface approaches) and those who gave the authors' words meaning in their own terms (deep approaches). Surface approaches to learning are characterized by a reproductive concept of learning that means that the learner is more or less forced to adopt a rote learning strategy. Deep approaches to learning are characterized by 'making sense', comprehending what is being said by an author in the text. Haggis (2002) has suggested that, over time, the focus on these approaches has resulted in assumptions being made that Marton and Säljö (1984) have described a highly significant set of relationships about how students learn. This, in turn, has resulted in the promotion of types of learning environments that are expected to enhance deep approaches to learning – in many cases, problem-based approaches. Although learners may change their approach according to their conception of the learning task, there is still an assumption that deep approaches are somehow necessarily better. As Haggis points out, many of these discussions about the promotion of 'deep approaches' avoid the paradox that a surface approach can lead to successful learning and that changing one's approach can be quite difficult.

Earlier work (Savin 1987) has also suggested that problem-based learning can promote progression through Perry's nine positions of how students' conceptions of the nature and origins of knowledge evolved (Perry 1970, 1988). In Perry's description of the attainment of intellectual and emotional maturity, the student moves from an authoritarian, polarized view of the world, through stages of uncertainty and accepting uncertainty, to an understanding of the implications of managing this uncertainty. Although such models have been helpful in assisting staff in higher education to take account of student cognition and development, there is little evidence to suggest that these typologies of learning help twenty-first-century students to learn more effectively. However, what the qualitative research in the field of problem-based learning demonstrates is that students' experiences of problem-based learning have been more meaningful and relevant to them and their lives than many lecture-based programmes they have experienced (Taylor 1997; Savin-Baden 2000a; Wilkie 2002). Given that students are increasingly being seen and managed as customers, and that both the public and private sector are demanding a critical workforce, perhaps it is the people, rather than the type of approach, that really matter.

Facilitating the development of criticality in the student

Many academics implement problem-based learning because they seek to provide for their students a kind of higher education which offers, within the curriculum, multiple models of action, knowledge, reasoning and reflection, together with opportunities for the students to challenge, evaluate and interrogate them. What they are seeking to do is not only to help students to be equipped for the world of work but to develop criticality in those students. The result is that problem-based learning is used as a means of helping students to challenge borders, construct knowledge and to evaluate critically both personal knowledge and propositional knowledge on their own terms. Thus students are expected to develop qualities of moral and intellectual as well as emotional independence, and are required to set their own goals and delineate their own processes for learning. This may not be said overtly by academics, but there is a sense that problem-based learning is being used for reasons that relate to something more than covering knowledge and being equipped for practice. There is a sense that staff want students to develop capabilities and the ability to manage knowledge in ways that will equip them for life. Goodlad (1995) has argued that staff need to promote self-confidence in students so that they are equipped to deal with uncertainty and conflict. The idea that students learn to deal with conflict in learning, in teams and between themselves and tutors, will help them to develop a criticality that they are unlikely to need to engage with if they are undertaking more traditional lecture-based forms of learning. However, not all staff and institutions will want to implement problem-based learning for these reasons. Their reasons may be more to do with finding a form of learning they believe will promote the widening of access to higher education and assist mature students. It might also be related to a desire to fulfil agendas guided by the work force development confederation that fund the education of health professionals or the concerns of professional bodies who guard entry into the professions. Yet world-wide the ability to help students develop such criticality in an increasingly fragmented global culture is one of the reasons why problem-based learning is being used to facilitate learning.

Facilitating the implementation of problem-based learning curricula

Facilitating problem-based learning can also refer to the ways staff implement problem-based learning in curricula. Staff generally design the curriculum using scenarios for learning but what counts as a scenario and the extent to which problem-based learning is used varies from programme to programme. The recent debates about curriculum design and what counts as a curriculum (Jackson and Shaw 2002) are important to the discussion about how such curricula are manufactured and these are discussed further in Chapters 9 and 10. However, in the context of the problem-based community, a community that in the main is experienced in developing materials for problem-based modules and programmes, the idea is that scenarios or problems are created by members of staff to prompt and inspire learning in the students. Through the development of this learning material, staff manufacture and project dramatic narratives in which students are expected to engage. Problems occur, however, in programmes where students do not aspire to understand the sub-text and the narratives, but see learning and assessment in terms of performative practices. Some of the difficulties here relate to the extent to which students are prepared adequately for problem-based learning.

Alternatively, obstacles emerge when students and tutors have different expectations of higher education. Thus what we see in practice is not only differences in problem-based learning that relate to the particular model of problem-based learning being implemented (Savin-Baden 2000a), but also differences that relate to the community into which it is placed. For example, it is often more difficult to analyse problem-based learning that is situated in just a module or a component of a programme, because the rhetorical artifacts (module descriptors, learning outcomes, materials) are smaller than when the whole programme is problem-based. Thus the meanings and views expressed in a problem-based module are held by the small community that designed the module (often in isolation from much of the rest of the programme), and thus the visions are less obvious, less spoken about and in some cases marginalized, because the shared views of this small community rarely extend across the whole staff group.

Facilitating educational development

Difficulties tend to arise in programmes for which educational development has not taken place to equip tutors for problem-based learning. Staff may feel ill-equipped and unsure about the purpose of problem-based learning and their role within it. This unease is not just because they feel unprepared to help students learn in this different way, but also because space has not been provided to enable the creation of a rhetorical community, so that there is little sense of vision and few opportunities for storytelling or the creating of communicative spaces. Educational development is vital to problem-based learning because it begins to help to formulate a community that has a rhetorical vision. During a period of staff development, tutors come together to begin to articulate their views, concerns and experiences and together they begin to create such a vision. Atkinson (2000) has suggested a series of processes that are important in the development of the ability to trust judgements that, while they have been researched in teacher education, have relevance here. During the formation of the ability to trust judgements, three components are deemed to be required: *support*, demonstrated in terms of positive and active interest; *direction*, the extent to which support for autonomy is provided;

and *structure*, a secure framework in which to reflect. Atkinson has suggested the following for why these three components are not forthcoming:

> Inappropriate support – if the result of trusting one's own judgment is always negative criticism or punishment

> Inappropriate direction – if one is never encouraged, or indeed allowed to act on one's own judgment, but always expected or compelled to follow the wishes and dictates of others

> Inappropriate structure – if the environment in which one performs one's actions is constantly shifting and throwing back unexpected responses
>
> (Atkinson 2000: 56)

It can be seen that inappropriate use of any of these three aspects can have an impact on students' ability to learn how to learn for themselves, value their own perspectives and feel that they have been enabled to take on responsibility for managing both team and individual learning. However, the difficulty here is deciding on what counts as appropriate and inappropriate in diverse subjects and contexts and to have some idea of how this informative but somewhat simplistic model can be applied to problem-based learning teams.

Facilitating effective assessment

One of the largest and longest debates about problem-based learning is that of assessment. For some, assessment issues in problem-based learning are no different than in other programmes and yet for other people there is a desire to see special types of assessment develop that fit specifically with problem-based learning. There are also debates about whether examination should be used and then subsequent discussion about what might count as an examination. However, what is important in such debates is that there *is* a realization that a fit is required between the types of learning encouraged though problem-based learning and the way in which it is assessed. Such interest also reflects that there is concern in the problem-based community for fairness and a shift away from hegemonic practices and the divisiveness of hints about how to formulate assessment scripts that inhibit symbolic convergence for both staff and students. Thus there is a move away from assessment as something that is seen as having divisive sub-text towards assessment that is aligned to the learning. What are rewarded are not answers that all follow similar plot lines, but instead those that demonstrate an ability to critique. Symbolic convergence does not demand agreement and thus students who present critical accounts expand the rhetorical vision through their work rather than undermining the vision it serves to strengthen. Thus one of the many important values that has emerged through the development of the problem-based community and the sharing of the rhetorical vision has been the repositioning of assessment as an important component of learning and the desire to encourage students to move away from strategic approaches and instead value assessment as personal development. What remains problematic about such idealistic visioning is that students working both to fund and attain a degree often do not share such a vision, and neither do the leaders of institutions, who are concerned that quality outputs are seen in terms of student degree standards and classifications. However, the desire to promote and develop effective and appropriate assessment through problem-based learning remains a laudable aim and a cause worth fighting for in the face of increasingly performative practices in higher education.

Facilitating tutor support

Although there are a number of initial educational development programmes available across the globe, as yet there is relatively little on-going support for staff involved in problem-based programmes. Many of the educational development programmes supplied by universities experienced in this approach to learning such as McMaster University, Canada and the University of Maastricht, Holland, are generic in nature and tend not to be able to help tutors deal with complex local concerns. Local support networks are proving to be successful, often within institutions but also across adjoining counties or states. Thus the initial programme of educational development may help to develop the problem-based community but long-term support groups are important both for facilitator development and for maintaining the importance and motivation for problem-based learning in the first few years of implementation. Tutor support may take the form of support groups serviced by an external facilitator or consultant, self-maintained support groups that are set up by the problem-based tutors themselves or the use of action learning sets. What is important about these groups is that they provide space for personal reflection, group support and a place where staff can discuss and manage any difficulties they are experiencing. Tutor support may also include the provision of master classes, in which a series of experts in problem-based learning or other related areas are asked to come to speak on a topic of interest. Such classes can take a variety of forms (see, for example, the suggestions in Chapter 6). However, what is important is that such sessions are not lectures followed by a few questions, but rather locations of debate and discussion where issues are grappled with.

'Becoming' a facilitator

There is often a feeling when one tries to implement problem-based learning and attends a facilitator training workshop that becoming a facilitator of this form of learning is different from other modes of facilitation. It is easy to argue that it is different, because facilitating problem-based learning promotes a different starting place for learning from more traditional approaches, both for the students and the teacher. For students, problem-based learning requires that they begin not only with an examination of what it is they need to know and find out to engage with the problem set before them, but also they are challenged to examine their assumptions about learning, knowledge and their position in the learning process. For the teacher, the starting place for learning is not problem-based seminars, but a long way before that in the conceptualization of the place of problem-based learning in the curriculum, their views about what counts as a curriculum and their assumptions about what counts as valid knowledge and the way in which problem situations are constructed. When staff engage with such debates before problem-based learning is to be introduced to their programme, it helps them to explore their often taken-for-granted assumptions about facilitating learning. As we have seen, the literature on facilitation tends to characterize facilitation through categories and generalize these across contexts. Yet the idea of facilitation in problem-based learning is embedded in this notion of 'becoming', as Day and Hadfield have argued:

> teachers learning about teaching is through a mixture of formal training, personal experiences, reading materials, advice from other teachers, and the transference of ideas and understandings from their personal lives and biographies. This has resulted in the content of their professional theories and the architecture of their professional selves. . . . becoming discontinuous and fragmented
>
> (Day and Hadfield 1996: 149)

The task of the facilitator is thus necessarily ambiguous, and, therefore, the articulation of it as a role demands that we engage with the tensions, dilemmas and risks implicit in it. However, it would appear that what we need to explore is not what constitutes a clear role for a facilitator, but the nature of the boundaries between teaching and facilitation, since the notion of 'role' in facilitation is contested ground. Facilitation is not about procedures or rules, but about creating different possibilities for learning, particularly ones that resist reductionist accounts and techniques for becoming. Thus we do not have types of facilitators, such as gap fillers, guides or direction givers. Instead, we have tutors in higher education who speak of the relationship between facilitation and the other types of teaching in which they are involved, in terms of overcrowded and often conflicted positions in which uneasiness about their identities, boundaries and relationships with students are evident. Thus facilitation has a plurality of boundaries and roles where previous beliefs and practices become vulnerable. The ways in which these are dealt with affect the interactional and pedagogical stances adopted by tutors through the life-course of facilitating a problem-based learning team. Furthermore, given the many discussions about what it means to be a professional teacher in higher education, Rappaport's view of the dilemma of contemporary professionalism can also help to examine the ambiguous nature of being a 'professional' facilitator:

> What we require is a model which allows us to play within the dialectic and to pursue paradox, first to one side, then the other one: one which allows us to welcome divergent reasoning that permits many simultaneous, different and contradictory answers, rather than a single solution or every special approach.
>
> (Rappaport 1981: 16)

Modes, models and approaches to facilitation

It could be suggested that facilitation in problem-based learning is different because the starting place for learning is different, the focus is on students' learning rather than the achievement of a specific task and there is a delicate balance between task and process in this form of learning. Yet to argue that facilitating problem-based learning is different from facilitating other types of team- or group-based learning is too simplistic. Heron (1989, 1993) has suggested three modes of facilitation that are useful for helping novice facilitators to consider how they operate:

1. *The hierarchical mode.* The facilitators direct the learning process and exercise their power over it. Thus they decide (however covertly) the objectives of the team, challenge resistances, manage team feeling and provide structures for learning. In short, the facilitators take responsibility for the learning that takes place.
2. *The co-operative mode.* The facilitators share their power over the learning with the team and enable the team to become more self-directed by conferring with them. The facilitators prompt the team members to decide how they are going to learn and how they are going to manage confrontation. Although the facilitators share their views, they are not seen as final but as one view among many.
3. *The autonomous mode.* The facilitators respect the total autonomy of the team; the facilitators do not do things for them or with them but give them the space and freedom to do things their own way. Without guidance, reminders or assistance, the team evolves its learning and structure, finds its own ways to manage conflict and gives meaning to personal and team learning. The facilitator's role is that of creating conditions in which students can exercise self-determination in their learning.

These modes are not designed to be discrete or hierarchical and do, to some extent, overlap with one another. However, although these are useful guides, particularly when coupled with the further dimensions that Heron has added, they do not in reality help us to understand what it means to become a facilitator. Problem-based learning is used in a host of ways in diverse curricula and thus how it is facilitated depends upon the context, the type of curriculum and the model of problem-based learning adopted. However, there are several issues about the process of 'becoming' a facilitator that are important to raise here. The dilemma in discussing what it means to become a facilitator in problem-based learning is in reducing it to a singular meaning while simultaneously inflating it with an improbable importance. If we are to start from the argument posited earlier that facilitating problem-based learning can be seen as different from facilitating other forms of group- and team-based learning, then it is likely that the processes involved in becoming a problem-based learning facilitator also have differences. However, there is a danger here in that arguing for such differences can result in a tendency to express what it means to be a facilitator in terms of definitive lists of competences. Recent studies have indicated that there are 'approaches' to facilitation that emerge through programmes that utilize problem-based learning. It is not possible to discriminate whether these approaches are the result of the use of problem-based learning *per se* or whether they will in fact be present in programmes that use small group learning of other sorts in a similar way. What is important about such approaches is that they are not seen as 'styles' of facilitation that outline desirable and less desirable behaviours. Nor should they be seen as the ability to facilitate problem-based learning teams successfully or unsuccessfully. Instead, it is evident that facilitator approaches change over time and with experience, and that they are affected by the problem-based team and the context in which problem-based learning is taking place (e.g. Silen 2001; Wilkie 2002).

In earlier work, I delineated Dimensions of Learner Experience, a framework that emerged from a study of teachers' and students' experiences of problem-based learning across disciplines and educational environments. What emerged from the research and the subsequent process of data interpretation was a means of structuring data through three concepts that I termed personal stance, pedagogical stance and interactional stance. These interrelated concepts emerged from people's experience of problem-based learning and together they encapsulated a multi-faceted view of learner experience (Savin-Baden 2000a). The main focus of this work was students' experience, but a more recent study (Savin-Baden 2002) sought to confirm or challenge the findings of this previous work. The stances are defined briefly as follows:

- *Personal stance:* the ways that tutors and students see themselves in relation to the learning context and how they give their own distinctive meanings to their experience of that context.
- *Pedagogical stance:* the ways tutors see themselves as teachers and students see themselves as learners in particular educational environments.
- *Interactional stance:* the ways tutors operate and the ways students work and learn in problem-based learning teams and how tutors and students construct meaning in relation to one another.

The findings of the more recent study (Savin-Baden 2002) are presented in Chapter 3 but what became apparent in the first cycle of data collection was that tutors' pedagogical stances affected the kinds of facilitation they offered and the types of learning behaviour they affirmed and rewarded in problem-based learning teams. The choices and interventions that tutors make within a learning environment and the particular learner history they bring to a learning environment all emerged from their pedagogical stances. Tutors' stances emerge from their prior learning experiences and their often taken-for-granted notions of learning and teaching. The four domains within the concept of pedagogical stance are: reproductive pedagogy, strategic pedagogy, pedagogical autonomy and reflective pedagogy. It is important to note that the borders of the domains merge with one another and, therefore, shifts between domains represent transitional areas where particular kinds of learning and teaching occur.

The reproductive pedagogy domain. In this domain tutors see themselves as the suppliers of all legitimate knowledge; anything less will result in inefficiency in their role as tutor and risk and failure for their students. The pedagogical stance in this domain is, therefore, characterized by the adoption of methods of teaching that maintain the *status quo* both for the student and in relation to the learning context.

The strategic pedagogy domain. Tutors in this domain offer students different learning strategies, but these are all within the limits of what is acceptable to the authorities (the institution, tutors and the profession). Pedagogical stance is characterized by tutors employing tactics that prompt cue-seeking behaviour in students (Miller and Parlett 1974). For example, they may use Socratic methods to help students to seek out cues.

The pedagogical autonomy domain. Tutors in this domain offer students kinds of learning opportunities that will give them a means of meeting their own personally defined needs as learners while also ensuring that they will pass the course. Tutors here see themselves as orchestrators of opportunities and strive to provide environments in which students can be independent in making decisions about what and how they learn.

The reflective pedagogy domain. Staff in this domain see their role as enabling students to realize that learning is a flexible entity and to understand that there are other valid ways of seeing things besides their own perspective. Staff thus help students to see that knowledge is contingent, contextual and constructed, and they understand themselves and their students as reflexive projects.

If we consider these domains in relation to the models of problem-based learning delineated in Savin-Baden (2000a), it is possible to see that particular pedagogical stances may influence the models of problem-based learning on offer. Thus tutors will need to recognize and explore their own pedagogical stances to examine the impact they have on the learning context and the problem-based learning team. It is important to note that even if the overall curriculum framework appears to reflect one of the models suggested below, staff can still operate a different mode within their own problem-based learning team through the imposition of their pedagogical stance on the way in which the team are expected to or allowed to learn. For some members of the team, this will result in disjunction, but as we shall see in Chapter 3, where stances are overtaken by the notion of tutors 'positioning themselves', it suits other students.

Model I: Problem-based learning for epistemological competence

Model I is characterized by a view of knowledge that is essentially propositional, with students being expected to become competent in applying knowledge in the context of solving, and possibly managing, problems. Knowledge is seen as being certain and the solutions to the problems are already known by the staff and known to be specific by the students. Problem-based learning is, therefore, used as a means of helping students to learn content. Thus problem situations are seen as the means by which students become competent in knowledge management and cover the required content in the curriculum. In a programme where this is the dominant model of problem-based learning, staff will, in general, be expected to operate within the domain of reproductive pedagogy. Some may opt for strategic pedagogy but this is likely to be undertaken covertly and will be seen as subversion because they are helping their problem-based team by offering guidance hints. This will be seen by other staff and students to be an unfair practice within this curriculum framework.

Model II: Problem-based learning for professional action

This model of problem-based learning has, as its overarching concept, the notion of 'know-how'. Action is seen here as the defining principle of the curriculum, whereby learning is both about what it will enable students to do and about mechanisms that are perceived to enable students to become competent to practise. Through this process of problem-based learning, students learn how to problem-solve and to become competent in applying this ability to other kinds of problem scenarios and situations within given frameworks. Reproductive pedagogy will also be paramount in this model, but in a different way. The focus will not wholly be on covering ground and reproducing knowledge. Here, the emphasis will be on reproducing skills effectively, but underpinned by the right knowledge. Being competent to practise will involve being able to reproduce not only the correct knowledge and skills but also the kinds of attitudes that are seen by the facilitators as appropriate for professional life.

Model III: Problem-based learning for interdisciplinary understanding

In this model of problem-based learning, there is a shift away from a demand for mere know-how and propositional knowledge. Instead, problem-based learning becomes a vehicle to bridge the gap between the know-how and know-that and between the different forms of disciplinary knowledge in the curriculum. In practice, staff in general adopt strategic pedagogy because it allows them the opportunity to develop in their students a form of understanding that is inter-disciplinary, both across forms of propositional knowledge and in the sense of using meta-skills across the boundaries between the world of work and the academic context. Some may still opt for reproductive pedagogy in an attempt to enable students to develop the knowledge and skills required and a few may opt for reflect-ive pedagogy because they want students to see that knowledge is contextual.

Model IV: Problem-based learning for transdisciplinary learning

In this model, problem-based learning operates in a way that enables the students to recognize that disciplinary boundaries exist but that they are also somewhat illusory, that they have been erected. Students might transcend boundaries but they are unlikely to challenge the frameworks into which disciplinary knowledge is placed. Here, tutors will encourage students to develop their own stance towards knowledge but without risking the re-framing of the infrastructure of the disciplines. The result is that tutors will largely adopt the pedagogical autonomy domain, since they can offer students flexibility in learning but also a means of ensuring that they will pass the course. Tutors will keep students within the disciplinary boundaries while also pointing out that they are illusory and, therefore, they will encourage students to be independent in making decisions about what and how they learn but within the boundaries.

Model V: Problem-based learning for critical contestability

This form of problem-based learning seeks to provide for the students a kind of higher education that offers, within the curriculum, multiple models of action, knowledge, reasoning and reflection, together with opportunities for the students to challenge, evaluate and interrogate them. Students will, therefore, examine the underlying structures and belief systems implicit within a discipline or profession itself, not only to understand the disciplinary area but also its credence. They will transcend and interrogate disciplinary boundaries through a commitment to explore the sub-text of those disciplines.

For students who adopt this model within their team, beyond the influence of the facilitator, then the facilitator is likely to feel deeply threatened. Even if the facilitator is able to move into working within the reflective pedagogy domain, the threat may be such that he chooses to retreat into a safer domain with clear boundaries such as reproductive pedagogy. The difficulties with this model largely stem from issues of power and control in the learning context. Staff sense of self is likely to feel at risk or threatened in their role in the team and in relation to their conceptions of learning and knowledge, since they will be under increasing scrutiny from the students. However, for some facilitators there will be a desire to operate in the reflective pedagogy domain, since they will want to encourage students to see that knowledge is contingent, contextual and constructed. Such tutors will see both themselves and the students within the team as reflexive projects.

Conclusion

This chapter has considered what can be meant by facilitation in problem-based learning. It can be seen as the facilitation of student learning, the formulation of curricula, the educational development of staff or all of these and more. What is important is that facilitation is not seen and defined as something that is structured and bounded, but is seen as a transitional process. Staff experiences of 'becoming' facilitators is an area that to date has been little researched and it is to this that we turn in the next chapter.

Part 2

On Becoming a Facilitator

3

Role Transitions: From Lecturer to Facilitator

Introduction

Part 2 explores notions of problem-based learning and facilitation from staff and students' perspectives. This chapter is based on my experience of being a consultant to a range of departments implementing problem-based learning and a four-year study that was undertaken to illuminate staff perspectives on their role and experience as facilitators on a programme that used problem-based learning. The chapter begins by setting the context for the research and then demonstrates the transitions staff have made personally and pedagogically when moving from the role of lecturer to that of facilitator.

Staff transitions: from lecturer to facilitator

For many staff engaged in problem-based learning, the transition from lecturer to facilitator demands revising their assumptions about what it means to be a teacher in higher education. This is a challenge to many, since it invariably demands recognition of a loss of power and control when moving towards being a facilitator. For many staff, becoming a facilitator is a daunting experience because although they may have taught students through workshops and small-group sessions, their role as a facilitator in problem-based learning often requires more of them than these other forms of teaching. This is because for many tutors it involves letting go of decisions about what students should learn, trusting students to learn for themselves and accepting that students will learn even if they have not been supplied with a lecture or handout. The conflict for many staff is in allowing students to manage knowledge for themselves, when in previous roles and relationships with students they have invariably been the controllers and patrollers of knowledge. Research into the role of the facilitator is growing, as we saw in Chapter 1. However, it is clear that understandings about the challenges and costs of being a facilitator in problem-based learning are seldom acknowledged.

The context of the four-year study

The research was undertaken in the new School of Nursing and Midwifery at a university that I will refer to as Curbar University. The new school was created from two existing colleges of nursing and midwifery in the final phase of the transfer of nurse/midwife education into higher education. The higher education institution had no previous links with either college and had had no nursing department prior to the integration. Re-validation of the programmes took place within 18 months of the transfer and utilized problem-based learning as a major teaching strategy. The shift towards problem-based learning was being undertaken at the same time as a number of other important changes that were occurring professionally and organizationally. Nursing and midwifery curricula in the early 1990s in the UK tended to be largely subject-based, lacking not only integration with practice but also the development of critique in students. A strategic review of the nursing and midwifery curriculum at Curbar had been undertaken to assist in the development of the new curriculum and these concerns regarding integration, critique and knowledge management were highlighted through this process.

To prepare the tutors for problem-based learning, a series of workshops had taken place between 1996 and 1998 and I had been the consultant who had planned and implemented this programme of staff development. Having worked with a group of 60 facilitators over a three-year period, helping them to design materials, to adapt assessment and providing facilitator support days, I was keen to follow their progress over the first three to four years. I was aware that to date there had been little in-depth research that had explored how staff both gained and developed their experiences as facilitators of problem-based learning. The research was therefore undertaken between 1998 and 2002 with a group of over 20 of the staff who were from diverse backgrounds in the field of nursing and midwifery. Although all the lecturers possessed a formal teaching qualification, none had experience of problem-based learning. These staff initially defined themselves as nurses, midwives, lecturers, clinical teachers and demonstrators in clinical skill laboratories. Such diverse roles with different philosophies prompted pedagogical conflict for the staff involved in their transition from and across their roles in the process of becoming facilitators.

Methods

I chose to use collaborative and narrative inquiry because it allowed the research to be exploratory and reflexive. This research design allowed for the development of collaborative relationships with the participants of the inquiry while also inviting reflexivity and critique. The data were collected through one-to-one in-depth interviews, informal and email discussion and post-interview reflections.

Validity, trustworthiness or honesty?
Trustworthiness in qualitative research has been discussed by many who offer schemes to ensure validity within this paradigm (Reason and Rowan 1981; Lincoln

and Guba 1985; Denzin and Lincoln 1994). Although I sought validity through personal reflexivity, collaboration between researcher and participants, triangulation and member-checking, I was aware that often we concentrate on research methods, ways of doing interviews, types of sampling and forms of credibility, so that instead of our values becoming explicit they become obscured by a sort of proceduralness that creeps into the research process. Thus the importance of reflexive practices lies in developing awareness and 'honesties' in the research process (Savin-Baden and Fisher 2002). My own involvement as a consultant meant that I had already become part of the facilitator development process and thus I sought to develop reflexive practices that helped me to highlight the ways in which our selves, our stances and our honesties can shift and change in relation to participants and their stories. Ensuring credibility in interpretation through the negotiation of meaning necessitated going beyond the mere recycling of transcription and description and engaging in critical discourse about my findings and interpretations with those involved. I analysed the data using interpretative interactionism, a poststructural interpretative style producing rich accounts that illuminate experience (Denzin 1989). My initial data analysis explored and identified common themes. I performed inductive analysis of transcripts of the interviews and critical discussion with participants to reflect on and examine current theory (Savin-Baden 2000a) and explore emerging theories. Using these data, I aggregated emergent themes from both analyses to provide robust explanations and ultimately to produce rich, illuminative accounts. Credibility in interpretation was important for developing *communitas*, a notion of shared meaning and discourse, particularly across diverse life worlds. The concept of life world is taken from Habermas (1989) and maintains that as human beings we have a culturally transmitted stock of taken-for-granted perspectives and interpretations that are organized in a communicative way. Thus, challenges to our life worlds may be at odds with, or bear little relationship to, our current meaning systems, ultimately prompting transitions in learning and our lives. Ensuring credibility in interpretation meant that the negotiation of meaning must go beyond the mere recycling of transcription and description, and thus the participants shared their perspectives on the construction of data as text.

Findings

In the early phase of data collection, tutors spoke of their transitions from lecturer to facilitator using a variety of metaphors, but over the course of the study there was a considerable shift from their early perceptions and experiences to those they held later when they had become more accustomed to facilitating problem-based learning teams. For example, to begin with, tutors saw themselves as novice facilitators whose role it was to control and direct the team, fill in the gaps in the students' knowledge base and ensure that the course content was covered. Although this was not the case for all facilitators, it was the case for most. There was, however, a small group who saw themselves more as guides. As guides they would help the team process along, offer hints and tips and be the safety net for the team. Many facilitators who were initially gap fillers became guides. The shifts made by staff were perceived by them to be related to the students shifting from critical thinking to critique and thus they became facilitators of knowledge acquisition and understanding, rather than givers of knowledge. This kind of shift was characterized by remarks such as, 'it was more a case of sitting back' and 'I feel now that facilitation is more about just being yourself in the team'. These kinds of reflections suggest that the move to being an expert facilitator was connected to shifts in pedagogical stances (Savin-Baden 2000a, 2002; Savin-Baden and Wilkie 2001), as well as the ways in which they positioned themselves in problem-based learning.

Initially, I had thought that the tutors' approaches to facilitation would predominantly reflect their pedagogical stance and that my findings would reflect the issues related to disciplines relatively new to the academe, which were also rigid, traditional and densely populated with women. Yet having shared these findings in international settings, there was a consistent resonance with this model. Over the course of the four-year study, I realized that, although tutors' stances did impact upon their overarching approach as a facilitator, what seemed to be pivotal was the way in which they 'positioned' or 'placed' themselves. Thus in this sense the notion of how tutors positioned themselves does not displace their pedagogical stance but rather *overlays* it. Positioning, then, is relational and can be affected by several factors. How staff position themselves as facilitators changes over time and also in relation to the problem-based teams they are facilitating, as well as possibly other things they are undertaking in their lives (such as a higher degree).

(Dis)placed academic

The idea of a (dis)placed academic captures the feeling that problem-based learning tutors are no longer strongly located in one discipline or branch of nursing but instead have to work inside and outside their area of expertise. For many, this dislocation brought confusion and discomfort. The result was that the tutors were simultaneously placed and displaced in the problem-based learning context. They were staff who were ambivalent about their new role and so although they valued being a facilitator, they struggled with their change of role. These tutors valued the freedom associated with encouraging students to be autonomous but they were not always entirely sure just how much autonomy they should allow. Thus the tutors saw autonomy as allowing the students to become self-directed in what and how they learned, but how much autonomy to allow was a major concern. Steve was a lecturer in the child branch of the programme, who was a curriculum planner and experienced teacher working predominantly with small groups. He felt that he had been in an ideal position to encourage and facilitate the introduction of problem-based learning into nursing and midwifery curricula since the strategic decision was made in 1996. Yet despite his commitment to problem-based learning, like several other facilitators he was uncertain about how much control to give the students:

> I'm sure everybody's different and I think that's okay because to begin with I think, we've been told how to do this style. This is the PBL [problem-based learning] style we're supposed to use – you stand back and let the students lead

and sometimes that's okay but sometimes it's – you have to use your own judgement of how effective the group are and how, the speed they are working through the stuff, then maybe you have to be comfortable in that role, take stock and look at what they are doing and maybe do a bit of direction. Believe me, in this instance, there isn't a lot of mileage in going up that particular avenue at the moment, it may be something that we will come back on, these areas, and if there are blind alleys within that, then fair enough, but be confident enough to do that, not let the group disappear off into every avenue they perceive as being relevant at that time because they don't, they really don't have the time for that.

The issue of students not having time to explore other areas emerged as an area of conflict for many staff. The struggle about how much self-direction they could safely allow students seems to have emerged from the discrepancies they felt between the ideals of self-directed learning in the adult learning literature and their perceptions of themselves as responsible teachers and professional nurses who needed to ensure students would be safe and competent practitioners.

Simon was a member of staff who was involved in multiple forms of teaching and learning. He had been given the overall remit of implementing curriculum change towards problem-based learning, and at the same time was implementing technological learning. His background in mental health nursing led him to believe that working and learning through a variety of approaches was useful and he assumed that as a facilitator he would not be particularly directive:

I didn't think for a minute that my normal teaching style was going to be okay as a problem-based learning facilitator, but I thought like many others do, that I do a lot of those things anyway. I ask a lot of questions, but it isn't until you actually think about being a facilitator, it's not just about asking questions, it's about the type of questions that you ask. And are the questions that you ask sufficiently open and non-directive to allow your students to think about issues and to find direction for themselves? So that I think I was just surprised about how much of a change was required of me. I thought I was at a particular point on the imaginary line of change and suddenly I realized, 'well yeah, I am, but I've got a fair bit to go', before I'm facilitating in a way which is acceptable.

Simon realized that he needed to change his style to offer students more autonomy; he saw the shift he needed to make as the difference between directing and guiding. Unlike Steve, he acknowledged that he was often directive and needed to change his position in relation to the students, so that he no longer felt he needed to provide students with a lot of information and was able to leave them to discover information for themselves.

(Re)positioned academic

Staff in this theme saw problem-based learning as offering them a positive opportunity to reposition themselves as tutors. Many of these had been uncomfortable with the role of traditional lecturer and facilitation offered them circumstances in which they could realign their pedagogical stances with their view of themselves as enablers of learning. In the main, staff in this theme not only repositioned themselves but also wanted to reposition the students by offering them greater power over what and how they learned. However, there were staff who did not do this. Such staff seemed as if they had repositioned themselves to promote student autonomy but in fact had not. This theme comprised three sub-themes, all related to the notion of repositioning: repositioned to maintain control, repositioned to offer control and repositioned to relinquish.

(Re)positioned to maintain control

Jack presented a picture of one whose values would initially seem to be as a repositioned academic, but in fact the values in use illustrated a need to be in control of knowledge. When I first spoke to Jack he argued that there was not enough flexibility within the nursing profession about what was to be valued and what counted as knowledge. He found it difficult to discuss problem-based learning separately from his perspective on life and saw students engaging with learning as a life-process. He believed that students should, at every level of the programme, be encouraged to question the knowledge, skills and ethical principles laid before them and to challenge the *status quo*. Thus Jack saw knowledge as something that was to be challenged and explored not only within the framework of the university, but also within practice and across the culture of practice and higher education. His main concern was that the underlying principles of problem-based learning were only being contained within components of the curriculum. He felt that staff and students would experience less disjunction and a greater sense of integration within their stances if problem-based thinking were to be more deeply integrated in the organizational structure. However, a year later it became apparent that the views he had first spoken of were not espoused in the practices of problem-based learning he adopted:

> I try not to be directive, although at times I say to the group, 'I think I'm taking my problem-based learning hat off for a few minutes, is that okay', so they know the difference, 'now I'm putting on my nursing lecturer's hat' and I will throw something out to them which is possibly a gaping hole in their argument and they should have identified it, so I will give it to them. Now go back and play with that ball, and I'll put that problem-based learning hat back on again. I think I'm that kind of facilitator, not directive, give them a long lead, do a lot of listening, try to play the game they want to play as long as they look at the objectives of the problem-based learning, and they are heading in that direction. I'm quite happy to believe that there are many different routes to achieve the learning outcomes, you don't have to go down a specific road, as long as at the end of the problem-based learning they have achieved them, for the students and for the patients.

Jack's perception of himself as not being directive does not square with 'putting on my nursing lecturer's hat' so that he can supply students with the practical knowledge they need to be safe with patients and achieve the learning objectives.

Repositioning for control here is seen in the values that Jack demonstrates in practice – he no longer wants students to challenge the *status quo*, instead he wants to ensure they are heading in the right direction and they have acquired the right knowledge, skill and capabilities for practice. Although this view in many ways is ethically sound and illustrates a desire to equip students well, Jack's narrow facilitation practices are likely to prevent the possibility of developing the kinds of criticality he first espoused.

In the other two sub-themes, staff repositioned themselves by promoting in students the development of autonomy. Many of the staff in these sub-themes were those who enabled students to develop towards a position of pedagogical autonomy and who often defined themselves as co-learners or members of the problem-based learning team.

(Re)positioned to offer control

Staff here repositioned themselves to promote self-direction in students. However, although they offered control, sometimes they did not then give it to the students and at other times the students chose not to take that control even though it was offered.

Neil was a lecturer in mental health and adult nursing, who had worked in several institutional settings and said he enjoyed the move to problem-based learning. To begin with he felt that this was just because it was a change in teaching style, but later he valued it in terms of the challenges it brought for him personally and pedagogically. He explained:

> I don't know how to put it, you don't see yourself as a teacher, you don't see yourself as a lecturer, yours is a different role. You have expertise in the area that you work, but it's not teaching, you are not really here to do teaching, you are here teaching outside the frame. I find it rewarding in the way that, you know, you see the student moving on, you see the student buzzing, you know, but in terms of me giving, that's one thing I don't know, what do I give?

In a later interview, Neil still did not see himself as a teacher, but his position had moved towards seeing himself more in partnership with the students in the learning process

> . . . and quite a few times I have seen myself almost as the student, you know, I was learning from them and I wouldn't say that it was something that I found surprising, you know, because the way problem-based learning is . . . and you know I would be picking up from them and sometimes afterwards ask them for copies of the pieces of work they have presented, which actually made them aware that you know, it's their work.

Neil repositioned himself both in relation to the teaching approach and in relation to the students. He saw himself as an enabler of learning and a learner.

(Re)positioned to relinquish control

Staff in this sub-theme sought to encourage both collaborative and *dialogic learning* so that students developed their ability to use dialogue, discussion and prior experience to enhance their learning. Tutors' concerns here were in relinquishing control to students so that autonomy was not just espoused but was played out in practice.

Sally was a member of staff who had been working with postgraduate students for many years and first described herself as being someone who was initially a (dis)placed academic. She had described herself as a non-directive facilitator, but the accounts she offered of what she did when facilitating her problem-based learning team indicated the dilemmas of being displaced in this context. Initially when I spoke to her, she was operating as a (dis)placed academic: she felt at odds with this approach to learning because she believed that being a good teacher meant she needed to ensure that students did not have gaps in their knowledge base. For her, failing to point out the gaps was irresponsible and she was not prepared to wait to let students discover the gaps for themselves in the weeks ahead, in case they missed them and then that would be her fault (not theirs). Yet two years later she was repositioned as someone who wanted to relinquish control and be a responsible facilitator, but also she felt her role as a tutor no longer included directing students. She explained:

> We still have arguments about this as PBL facilitators, you still hear people saying 'I have done all this preparation for this trigger, it took me hours to do this', and I am still saying to them, 'Why? You are not doing these triggers, your group is doing this trigger'. So I would say to them as a facilitator, 'read it, make sure you understand where you are trying to go with your group with it, but don't go and prepare work for it because that is not your job. That is the job of the group. Your job is there to try and help them see the way that they've got to go with it, and if you're preparing stuff it may not be what they need to know'. So I would be saying to someone, 'yes don't go and get the trigger out of the cupboard just as you walk into the class', you know [laughs] and I have been guilty of that a couple of times and it doesn't work. And I've been guilty of that when I've thought, 'oh it's that trigger again, this is the third time I've had this trigger I am okay with it', you go and get it and somebody has changed it. Oh, whoops, wait a minute [laughs]. So I think be well-prepared when you go into class, but only be prepared to facilitate the group, not be prepared to teach them what the trigger is telling them, and I think that that is really, really important, because it is sometimes easy to lose sight of the fact that we aren't there to teach in the conventional sense of the word but certainly that is something I have thought of saying to somebody.

(Dis)located academics

Staff in this theme were spoken about by other tutors. There was only one member of staff I interviewed who could be classed in this category, who has been omitted for reasons of confidentiality. Many of the members of staff spoken of here were those who had either opted out of involvement with problem-based learning from the beginning, or had tried being a facilitator and then given it up, or used mechanisms to sabotage problem-based learning. These staff seemed to dislike problem-based learning because they felt that it did not accord them the same power and status as lecture-based forms of learning. Others felt dislocated because of the disjunction they experienced as a result of their role change, and ultimately chose to stop being involved with problem-based learning. Simon explained his frustration with staff who believed that didactic teacher-centred approaches were the only way to produce good nurses:

> Well, the rationale underpinning problem-based learning was explained to these people and they were – and attempts were made to engage them in dialogue about the rationale and the principles behind an alternative way of delivering biological science material ... The staff in that group are concerned that students won't acquire a sufficient volume of knowledge to enable them to be safe practitioners, and they operate on the belief that attendance at a lecture by a student equates with acquisition of that large body of knowledge, and they obviously believe that imparting a large body of knowledge to the student equates with learning.

Simon's frustration stemmed partly from the realization that he had sometimes been at the border of being very directive, but he also realized that these staff felt dislocated because they were no longer in charge of what was being learned and so they used controlling mechanisms to manage the team learning.

In contrast Ruth, one of several staff researching problem-based learning, had adapted easily to facilitation because it suited her pedagogical stance. She was frustrated with this group of peers but was a little more sympathetic than Simon. Ruth recognized that these staff felt dislocated because they believed they no longer had status because their expertise in particular areas was, they perceived, no longer valued by other staff or by students. She explained:

> There are one or two facilitators who have had difficulties with their groups and quite interestingly one of my colleagues was having a lot of difficulties with one of the first groups, and wasn't quite blaming the problem-based learning, but was saying that he felt it was the problem-based learning that was creating this, it wasn't suitable and the students couldn't manage it. He's got a group of the new intake and he is saying that they are just completely different, what they have done in their first two triggers is far, far more than one other person has said, who has stepped in for a buddy to take a group for them, he ran the group in such a completely different way, just couldn't hack it, got quite upset about it and had actually said to him that this was their group and they had decided that this was the way they were going to run it and they were not going to change it just because he was there. Whereupon the facilitator had got quite upset, saying 'you must do this and you must do that' and they said 'well why, we've been together for about a year, we're doing all right, why should we change it just because you're here?'

Issues of power and control in problem-based learning were ones that were spoken of many times. There was a sense that these staff were dislocated not just because problem-based learning did not fit with their personal or pedagogical stances, but also because they felt unable to let go. Letting go was partly about control, but it was also about feeling safe enough with this method of learning and feeling that students could be trusted. Many facilitators later remarked on how part of the transition they had made was learning to trust the students to learn for themselves. They reflected on how little they had trusted students and felt that their ability to trust them more had enabled students to become increasingly self-directed. Taylor (1997) covers issues of students' readiness for self-direction in problem-based learning, but there would also appear to be a parallel issue here for staff.

Commodifying academic

The migration into the academic world of strategic values that focus more upon achieving some externally validated end, rather than the validation of interactive and collaborative forms of learning and reasoning, is resulting in students focusing more on strategy and less on the values of process. Strategic values focus upon achievement and outcomes and upon innovation for profitability and survival. Commodifying academics are those who promote pragmatic responses to issues raised by practitioners – the result usually being only to encourage in students the valuing of practical knowledge, while downgrading the kinds of reasoning that encourage students to form their own ideas and judgements and to keep their own critical distance from all they experience within a course. Thus these tutors believe they should be enabling the development of mode 2 knowledge, rather than mode 1 knowledge (Gibbons *et al.* 1994). Mode 2 knowledge is knowledge that transcends disciplines and is produced in, and validated through, the world of work. Knowing in this mode demands the integration of skills and abilities to act in a particular context. Thus these tutors supply a context in which students can practise mode 2 knowledge in the university setting. The aim is to provide students with the kind of knowledge demanded not only by the health service and industry but also by students who demand to be given applied forms of knowledge (socially distributed knowledge). The result is not only the commodification of knowledge but also possibly the commodification of relationship between academics and students. Tutors see themselves as being there to help students get the right knowledge for practice and this often spills over into a co-dependency type of relationship as seen here with Kathleen in her first interview:

> I feel that I have probably tried very early on to be one of the group, as opposed to lead the group, and made it quite plain to them that I was only there if they couldn't come by any answers any other direction and I still think that. I don't think it's changed an awful lot. I probably talk less now than I did initially.
>
> *Do you see yourself differently now?*
>
> Only in the aspect that I feel that I know these students extremely well now, and they seem to feel as though they can talk to me about anything as well, which is quite useful and I can see the progress that they have made in the year,

far better than if I had just been going and teaching in the normal fashion, modified lectures or something. I actually get an awful lot more satisfaction out of seeing this group. There were three younger ones, the seventeen-year-old and two of the others who were both under twenty-one, very, very quiet when they first came in, they did not really have much confidence and had no opinions and as the year has progressed, they have blossomed and begun to be quite confident about what they are saying. There was a big difference in them, so the feedback for me as a teacher, is instant in problem-based learning, and I actually like that and to tell you the truth when they are out for their clinical placements and I haven't seen them for quite a while, I actually miss them because you get so accustomed to seeing them at regular intervals, that it's a long time between seeing them and then, I wonder how they are getting on.

Kathleen's desire to become one of the team at the outset emerged from her need to nurture the problem-based learning team and ensure that they would feel safe, competent and equipped before they went into practice. Her supportive relationship with students, while helpful to students, did not often promote autonomy and self-direction. Instead, Kathleen's need to care for her students resulted in a dependent parental relationship. Parenting students meant she modelled appropriate behaviour and use of practical knowledge which would be acceptable in practice settings. Although there are many advantages to problem-based learning, the development of co-dependent relationships between staff and students could not be said to be one of them, since it can result in too much personal disclosure by the facilitator and unnecessary risk to the team.

Karen's perspective was slightly different. She described herself as someone who had never liked the traditional lecturer role and had always felt more comfortable in seeing learning as a process of discussion. Although she was involved in a number of new innovations, problem-based learning was the one about which she spoke most enthusiastically. Her position reflected her belief that learning and life was a complex business and that her role was to help students to see and engage with these complexities. However, there were times when she overplayed the helping role and stifled the students' freedom. Although she recognized the need to move away from recipes for treatment, there were times during the interviews when the descriptions of the problem-based learning team verged on the edge of being some kind of therapeutic group:

> I think the students like it, again because they can bring up their problems whether it is to do with the trigger, the scenario, the discussions or whether it's to do with themselves within the college and the course . . .

Although it is important to acknowledge the interrelationship between learning and personal concerns, there were times when Karen's role as a nurse, helping people to get better and move on overflowed into 'caring' for students. However, Karen's view of learning as encompassing not just propositional knowledge but also personal knowledge was something which relates to the work of Jacobsen (1997). He argued that discussion about problems and issues beyond the problem-based learning team were vital to enable learning to take place. Jacobson termed these 'frame factors', issues that were raised by the students that do not relate directly to the problem scenario but are important to students. Examples that occurred on this research site included transport between campuses, the arrival of student uniforms and students' personal problems.

Managing transitions

Staff in this study seemed to receive little support or guidance in ways of managing transitions in the change process. Many of them found their self-management a complex task, while they were simultaneously helping students to manage their own transitions towards learning approaches that few had previously encountered. Although this was the case for most staff in this study, there were some who were not prepared to make shifts of any kind. However, facilitators valued support from each other and many facilitators commented that the support of other facilitators had been a major influence in adjusting to and developing problem-based learning. However, at the same time they experienced 'the complexities and tensions inherent in two major sources of identity, one local, visible and tangible, the other cosmopolitan, largely invisible and disembedded' (Henkel 2000: 19), in short their department and the university. Thus the institutions in which academics are located and position themselves ensure that knowledge production and transmission occur in particular and acceptable ways to both the profession and the academics while also sustaining the professional identities of academics. Yet at the same time, several challenges faced by most of the tutors are probably generalizable to all problem-based learning facilitators:

- the responsibility facilitators shoulder to enable student learning;
- the challenges for them as individuals when their prior experience has been about lecturing and giving advice;
- the shift they have to make in their conceptions of teaching and student learning in order to understand how to implement problem-based learning;
- the personal cost of having to deal with students in small teams, students who challenge, contest and are also possibly aggressive towards them;
- a sense of bereavement for a past role that they enjoyed and that has now largely ceased;
- staff unease with their new and changing role;
- the ways some staff feel empowered by problem-based learning but the way in which this results in tensions with others who do not;
- the way that some staff are expected to facilitate problem-based learning when this approach does not fit with their perceptions about teaching and learning;
- the tension staff experience between wanting to ensure that students are competent to practice but also that they are enabled to become independent inquirers;
- the way in which they are expected to manage multiple roles, including those to which they are ill-suited;

- the relatively poor organizational support staff receive if they are problem-based learning facilitators; there is a sense that if they are involved in problem-based learning, then that is their choice and they must accept the consequences;
- the lack of recognition within universities of the complexities for staff, personally and pedagogically, of implementing problem-based learning;
- the lack of preparation for problem-based learning that many facilitators experience.

Conclusion

To date, little has been documented about support and guidance for facilitators as they seek to manage complex team dynamics, their own evolving role and the increasing sophistication of the learners. While the research into facilitation in problem-based learning is increasing, relatively little has been done concerning facilitator preparation or tutors' pedagogical stances. Conceptions of facilitation are needed that take into account not only learning and learning contexts, but also the changing frameworks of knowledge both within and beyond the academe. Chapter 4 will examine the notion of being an effective facilitator and explore the extent to which effectiveness is a realistic expectation in the diverse and fragmented context of higher education.

4

Being an Effective Facilitator

Introduction

This chapter examines the notion of effective facilitation and explores the ways in which facilitation has been conceptualized in much of the research to date. It then explores current research and practices about what it means to become a facilitator in problem-based learning and questions the relationship between facilitation as teaching and facilitation as ecologies of practice. Students' experiences of facilitation are explored and ways of equipping students for problem-based learning are suggested. The final section of the chapter explores the position of power in facilitation and suggests how issues of power might be dealt with in the context of problem-based learning teams.

Effective facilitation?

In recent years, there has been increasing debate about whether facilitation is just a form of good teaching or whether it is something else (Boud and Miller 1996). As discussed in Chapter 1, there has been much philosophizing and relatively little research in this area. Such philosophizing has, until recently, resulted in research being undertaken into the facilitator role with relatively little real exploration of what is meant by facilitation, facilitator or the role of the facilitator by either researchers or participants in the research. This confusion is not only seen in the research but also in the way staff are equipped for implementing problem-based learning. For example, many staff undergo facilitator training programmes, but as yet there seems to be little distinction made between the different but overlapping roles. One way of engaging with this difficulty would be to argue for role distinctions such as team facilitator, problem-based learning tutor and programme manager. Equipping someone to facilitate a problem-based learning team (a team facilitator) is a task that requires fewer capabilities than the role of facilitating a team while also designing materials and other problem-based learning components of the curriculum (a problem-based learning tutor). A further role might be that of problem-based learning programme manager who designs the programme and oversees the implementation of problem-based learning but may or may not be a problem-based learning tutor or team facilitator as well. Although these roles do, to a large extent, overlap, the distinction is important when undertaking research into what might count as effective facilitation.

The difficulty with the notion of effectiveness in facilitation is that there is an implicit assumption that there are necessarily both right and better ways of facilitating problem-based learning teams. Although we can look to models of facilitation and question whether our role is that of a teacher, a tutor or facilitator and seek to define those roles, these models and arguments do not really move us along in terms of equipping us to enable students to learn through problem-based learning. As we have seen in earlier chapters, much of the research into facilitation begins not only from the standpoint of the teacher but also that of the researcher. For example, Gijselaers (1997) examined contextual factors on tutors' behaviours and the effects of departmental affiliation on tutoring. Quantitative analysis of data indicated that overall the level of stability in tutor behaviour, which was examined across different problem-based learning teams, was low, as was the generalizability. What was apparent from the study, although Gijselaers did not couch it in such terms, was that the team facilitator was affected by both the learners and the learning context. Dolmans *et al.* (1994a,b) have also sought to quantify team facilitator behaviours and effectiveness and such studies imply a sub-text about facilitation that has not been explored overtly in many of the quantitative studies. What I mean is that there appears to be an assumption that there are specific roles, attributes and ways of being that characterize facilitation that is 'good' or 'better' than others. Yet as Gijselaers (1997) discovered, much of what occurs in facilitating problem-based learning is related to the learners themselves. Thus the idea that facilitation is a specific kind of 'role' is in itself problematic. It is as if there is some kind of idea of constructing a false identity to prevent ourselves from becoming too subjective, too involved with students and their learning. Although it is perhaps inadvisable that the facilitator brings his own learning needs to the team discussion or attempts to create a culture of dependency in the team, to deny the inter-subjectivity of team and facilitator is somewhat naive. Facilitators and students influence one another in a variety of ways, such as their views about what counts as knowledge, the interplay of content and process and the ways in which they do and do not deal with conflict in the team. Facilitators and problem-based learning teams tend to shape and challenge each other, so while most teams will meet the learning objectives of the programme or module as a minimum, they will do so in different ways because of the team dynamics and the pedagogical stance and academic positioning of the facilitator. However, we must also be aware that the growing number of 'how to' and 'hints and tips' texts in higher education may make us feel a little safer as we set out on our journey to become facilitators, but in fact they do little in terms of helping us to examine the ways in which our own stances and positions as teachers affect and impact upon learners in problem-based learning.

Facilitation in problem-based learning demands not just awareness but a personal transitional process whereby we deeply critique the behaviours and actions we take up in the process of facilitating a problem-based learning team. For example, downplaying our knowledge as facilitator or dismissing it as irrelevant can widen rather than reduce the gap between teacher and learner. It is easy to imply we know little and thus imply we can be of little help to students. Many facilitators appear to oscillate between being directive towards students and saying very little at all. For example, many of them feel that for students to be competent and safe practitioners, they need to direct them towards the right information so that they cover the material the facilitators expect. Alternatively, facilitators new to problem-based learning often feel it is better to say less – or even nothing – so that the students feel that they are taking the lead in the learning. The first creates student dependency; the latter, particularly with students new to problem-based learning, results in students feeling that the lack of direction is duplicitous because they feel it is the facilitator's way of avoiding a declaration of their own agenda and concerns. Thus there needs to be a balance between these issues, so that the facilitator can be part of the team discussion in ways that the students themselves value. Not engaging in debate can be taken, by some students, as disinterestedness or a belief that the facilitator is not prepared to express their own opinion and thus remain a voiceless participant. Finding this balance is difficult. Facilitators have spoken of sitting on their hands, looking out of the window or mentally planning their social life while 'facilitating' a problem-based learning team. Such strategies were designed to prevent them from interfering with and directing the team, but instead resulted in a good deal of confusion for students who felt that their facilitator did not want to be there. Thus effective facilitation demands that we deconstruct the assumptions and practices of our pedagogies and that we are also prepared to have a voice and, where necessary, challenge students to raise issues. Weil and McGill have argued:

> The onus for raising . . . issues is also often put upon those who have the most to lose. For example, in largely male or white groups, it is common for members of oppressed groups to be seen as 'the problem', or as 'having a problem' that is not 'the group's' concerns . . . Equally when women or black people try to highlight aspects of their own experience, which may differ from that of others in the group, they can be seen as disrupting the status quo . . . prior educational and social experience has conditioned us to see engagement with such issues as 'disruptive' or 'divisive' and as somehow separate from the realm of experience considered 'legitimate' within personal growth and development contexts.
>
> (Weil and McGill 1989: 264–5)

The facilitator, therefore, has a role in not only being honest about her own agenda within the team, but also a responsibility to help the team to examine what counts as acceptable behaviour and perspectives and how notions of difference can be assimilated into the team effectively. It is, in many ways, easier to avoid engagement with complex issues that are perhaps seen as disruptive than it is to help students learn to manage them within the team. Facilitators need to be aware of such complexities so that they do not silence some and privilege others. Thus effective facilitation demands not only that we acknowledge and manage diversity, but also that we learn to trust the judgements and intuitions of ourselves, our colleagues and our students.

Intuition and facilitation

When you say the word 'intuition', people generally think that you are talking about either one's gut reaction to something or some kind of bizarre mystical practice. Teachers in higher education often talk about 'knowing' a session is going well or badly and they can also often articulate what it was that went correctly or incorrectly. Intuition is something that is difficult to pinpoint and there has been little research that has explored the nature or value of intuition in teaching. The work of Belenky *et al.* (1986) perhaps comes closest to exploring the notion of intuition in that they explored women's notion of 'knowing'. Belenky *et al.* examined the ways in which women see reality, described it from five different perspectives and from this drew conclusions about the way women see truth, knowledge and authority. In total, 135 women were interviewed, from diverse backgrounds, almost half of whom adopted subjective knowledge, a perspective from which truth and knowledge are conceived of as personal, private and subjectively known or intuited, as their stance. What Belenky *et al.* found was that these women's assumptions about intuition and private knowing were used as a guiding force for their understanding, yet when they were working and learning in the public domain, this guiding intuition was not valued or given any currency.

It is noticeable, too, that in the context of problem-based learning, little attention has been given to the role of intuition in facilitation. This would seem to be not only related to the ways in which our education systems have become outcome-based and benchmarking focused, but also because when there is a push to encourage strategic learning there is little place for the kinds of knowing that are often difficult to articulate and argue for. For example, in many curricula the focus on higher education for the world of work has meant that many students have become focused on doing less but wanting more. Arguments abound as to whether uploading handouts and detailed lecture notes on to WebCT or Blackboard is something that helps or hinders student learning. The customer culture has led many students to believe that they have a right to be given all the information supplied in a lecture as a handout. There appears, in some university programmes, to be little real sense of the notion of reading for a degree; the idea that students faced with a question, essay or problem-situation spend time exploring the literature and examining the evidence to come to a critical stance. The use of strategic approaches to passing assignments or wanting hints and tips on passing examinations may not be new but they are certainly on the increase and, as such, this does little to encourage students to take up a critical stance towards knowledge. Yet both staff and students' stories of their experience of problem-based learning suggest that intuition is very much part of the process of learning and facilitation. Facilitators I spoke with talked of knowing when the team was going well, but also of times when they were aware that there were difficulties in the team but could not define what the difficulties were or how they knew this.

Claxton (2000) defines intuition as 'immediate apprehension, without the intervention of any reasoning process' and has suggested that there are six types of intuition:

- *Expertise*: the unselfconscious and unpremeditated mastery of a complex domain, so that, for example, an expert teacher or clinician will adjust their actions with little thought or reasoning as to why they made those particular decisions in that particular context.
- *Judgement*: making accurate decisions without necessarily being able to justify them at the time.
- *Creativity and problem-solving*: the use of creative and unconscious processes to solve a problem.
- *Rumination*: the seeking of insight through reflecting on personal experience.
- *Sensitivity*: a heightened awareness to a situation that is both conscious and unconscious.
- *Implicit learning*: the acquisition of expertise through non-conscious under-standing and making use of patterns of information in complex contexts that are both unconscious and difficult to articulate.

Although many of these processes are evident in the strategies facilitators use when they make conscious or unconscious decisions in the process of facilitating problem-based learning teams, I would argue that they could not all really be classed as forms of intuition. Intuition in the context of facilitation would appear to demand the use of expertise but often in problem-based learning it takes time for facilitators to develop expertise. They may be experts in particular areas of discipline knowledge but not in facilitating problem-based seminars. Judgement could be said to be an intuitive process but again it may only emerge through experience, whereas the use of creativity and problem-solving would appear to be a vital intuitive process for problem-based learning facilitators, since it demands that they link together prior knowledge and understanding with current experience. Thus prior experience of small-group teaching along with managing complex team dynamics and the discussion of different types of discipline knowledge, all within the one problem-based learning seminar, will demand that facilitators are able to use creativity and problem-solving to link these processes and experiences together. As such, these could be classed as intuitive processes rather than intuition *per se*, as Eraut has argued:

> . . . intuitive processes themselves are easily recognizable. Who does not recall from their life experience examples of retrieval of knowledge from memory, insight through connecting different areas of knowledge, use of mental models and imagery, sensing new aspects of the situation, recognizing familiar patterns, rapidly finding a decision option to respond to a changing situation or problem?

> (Eraut 2000: 265)

I would argue, therefore, that rumination and sensitivity are part of intuitive processes as is implicit learning, rather than particular varieties of intuition as Claxton has suggested. Thus in the context of problem-based learning, the way in which intuition could be highlighted is through the development of expertise, judgement, creativity and problem-solving. These capabilities are ones that could be accentuated and fostered in both educational development workshops and facilitator support groups to enable the development of intuition for both staff and students.

Changing perspectives: facilitation as ecologies of practice?

There has been a shift since the late 1990s away from defining particular character-istics of facilitation towards an exploration of the complex interaction between team, facilitator and learning context. Facilitation is now no longer seen as just about forms of teaching or modes of facilitation, but instead it is rooted in ecologies of practice. Ecologies of practice (after Stronach *et al.* 2002) refer to experiences, beliefs and practices that professionals accumulate in learning and performing their roles. Such ecologies relate largely to the kinds of knowledge that are essentially intuitive or tacit and encompass particular ideologies that may be personally held, but in the main are held by a particular profession. Examples would include ideals such as students needing to be inducted into a profession through particular rituals and practices or ideologies about the values of client-centred practice, the need for propositional knowledge as a baseline for learning or convictions about the nature of good practice. It might be possible to apply some approaches to facilitation across different professions and disciplines and in so doing be able to locate the kinds of modes that are at play in a given discipline. Yet I would argue that the impact of the discipline itself is also important in terms of the kinds of facilitation on offer to students in a given subject area because of the particular ecologies of practice. Thus in practice what we would see in problem-based learning facilitation would be connected to the ecologies of practice within the discipline. While there would be some personal variations if we look at the expectations and experiences of facilitation in the literature, there are some general trends that have been exemplified by Kandlbinder and Maufette (2001), Silen (2001) and Wilkie (2002), who have sought to examine students' and teachers' perceptions and experiences of problem-based learning.

In Silen's (2001) work, notions of learning to be a nurse and making sure that students learned the correct knowledge for practice was evident in students' views of themselves as future nurses and the way that problem-based learning was implemented reflected both the nature of the discipline and the profession. This was also evident in a recent study by Wilkie (2002), who examined the strategies adopted by new facilitators in a problem-based learning programme and followed their progress for two years. The study was undertaken in a School of Nursing where the pre-registration programme utilized problem-based learn-ing as a major teaching strategy. Although all the nursing lecturers possessed a formal teaching qualification, none had experience of problem-based learn-ing. Participants represented a range of teaching experience, nursing practice backgrounds and teaching styles. Wilkie's findings indicate not only the adoption of four different modes of facilitation over time and the impact of six elements on these modes, but also that several of the issues regarding facilitation related to the professional identities of the lecturers involved. Wilkie found that although every facilitator had a unique style of facilitation, four approaches to facilitation were evident:

- directive conventionalist;
- liberating supporter;
- nurturing socializer;
- pragmatic enabler.

Wilkie also defined six further elements (content eliciting, process interventions, engagement, frame factors, narrative and evaluation) that impacted upon each approach and, despite all of the elements being present in each of the four approaches, they were used to different degrees and in different ways in each approach. What is important to note was that the approaches were neither fixed nor hierarchical. Instead, these approaches, like the concept of personal, pedagogical and interactional stances, were time- and context-bound. The approaches are as follows.

The directive conventionalist approach. In this approach, learning was content-focused and under the direction of the facilitator. Students were encouraged to seek out and learn facts. Aspects of problem-based learning, such as learning skills or promotion of critical thinking, were of less importance than factual content. The characteristic feature of the directive conventionalist approach was the use of convergent, directive questions to elicit content. The approach was associated predominantly with novice facilitators who may have selected it for reasons of familiarity with a lecturer role and feeling in control.

The liberating supporter approach. Facilitators who adopted this approach kept their intervention in the problem-based learning seminar to a minimum. Within the limits of the trigger, the students were free to decide on their own learning, in terms of both the content and learning method. Although there was some emphasis on encouraging students to acquire self-directed learning skills, the overall purpose of the learning was content acquisition rather than learning processes in their own right. This approach was adopted least often. It was the approach that most facilitators, at least in their initial experience of problem-based learning, perceived to epitomize problem-based learning facilitation.

The nurturing socializer approach. This approach was student-centred, nurturing and supportive. Both facilitators and students made extensive use of narrative. The approach was supportive, with facilitators believing that students had to feel valued to be able to value and care for patients.

The pragmatic enabler approach. This approach developed over time with increased exposure of facilitators to problem-based learning. It was not fully identifiable until the third cycle of the study when it had become the most common approach. The pragmatic enabler approach emphasized learning processes rather than content acquisition. Facilitators related to the requirement to produce qualified practitioners. To enable students to achieve their maximum potential, facilitators required a flexible approach, which was time- and context-dependent and responsive to the needs of a diverse range of students.

Wilkie's study not only demonstrates staff transitions over time and context, but also the nature of the discipline in such categories as the nurturing socializer. In this approach, staff were often seen to care for their students in the problem-based learning team in the same way that they had previously cared for their patients. The early approaches of staff to facilitation would also seem to reflect the nature of the discipline in that most staff, when they were novice facilitators, adopted the directive conventionalist approach to learning because it felt familiar and enabled them to feel that students had covered the right knowledge to ensure that they would be safe on the hospital wards. Such ecologies of practice can be seen in two other recent studies, in physiotherapy (Lahteenmaki 2001) and science teaching (Kandlbinder and Maufette 2001).

Kandlbinder and Maufette (2001) examined conceptions of teaching 'basic concepts' in sciences in programmes that used student-based learning approaches, including problem-based learning. Lecturers were screened to establish whether they had a more learner-focused approach to their teaching than other staff and in-depth interviews were conducted with these staff. The assumption was that lecturers who were more student-centred would design programmes that would facilitate effective learning. The findings indicate that student-centred teachers in the sciences had the same goals as their less student-centred colleagues, namely to ensure that students developed a thorough knowledge of the discipline by learning 'basic concepts' at the start of the course. What was particularly interesting about this study was the foundational view of knowledge, whereby the assumption was that students needed to learn and understand a given body of knowledge before they could progress to the next level of the course. However, Kandlbinder and Maufette argued that what many lecturers referred to as 'basic concepts' were in fact far from basic and what they appeared to be describing was a pedagogical representation of ecologies of practice. They argued that what emerged from the data were four descriptions of what basic concepts were meant to represent to the students. The metaphor of building was central to the notion of disciplinary understanding and knowledge was seen as the ability to test propositions rather than the learning of a body of knowledge through rote memorization. They argued:

> Basic concepts can also form the boundary of received knowledge, providing identity to the discipline. By their nature these concepts are a particular kind of knowledge that is difficult to locate ... In these cases science university teachers talk about finding the essence of the discipline, particularly in terms of the traditions of science.
>
> (Kandlbinder and Maufette 2001: 49)

The four descriptions they offer of these basic concepts are:

- *Pillars*: propositions that provide a sound foundation.
- *Boundary*: contains the knowledge of the discipline.
- *Web*: connects the knowledge of the discipline.
- *Model*: the concepts and their interconnections are tested against reality.

It is not clear whether these concepts are hierarchical, but it would appear that they represent an ecology of practice within the science disciplines, which, as Bourdieu (1975) has argued, have strongly differentiated power and status, tend to stand in competition with one another, and are 'the locus of competitive struggle' for individual scientists located within the fields: 'What is at stake is the power to impose the definition of science . . . best suited to [individual] specific interests' (p. 23). Such sites of struggle and power plays perhaps need to be explored in more depth by those using problem-based learning in science.

Students' experiences of facilitation

Relatively little research has explored students' experience of facilitation, although there appear to have been a number of studies that have examined their attitudes to problem-based learning or students' responses to particular innovations implemented to support problem-based learning, such as databases and online support materials. For example, Quinlan (2000) developed and evaluated a database for students in veterinary medicine. She found that the database helped students access relevant high quality articles but was not directive as to their use, so that students felt that they themselves could choose how to utilize the literature. However, some felt overwhelmed by the range of materials and found it difficult to prioritize their learning needs. This interesting study points up the fact that equipping students to be directed in a variety of ways is an increasing concern in the problem-based learning community.

Two other recent studies also support concerns reported earlier (Taylor 1997; Savin-Baden 2000a) about the nature of self-direction in problem-based learning and the role of the facilitator over time. Silen (2001) used ethnography to understand student-centred learning from the students' perspectives. She found that students' conceptions of responsibility and independence resulted in students seeing themselves on a continuum of frustration and stimulation. Students' view of their position along the continuum appeared to affect their willingness to engage with self-direction. However, what is particularly interesting about Silen's work is the way in which students managed the interrelationship between their own personal learning needs and those of the curriculum. Students' ability to be independent learners as opposed to dependent ones was affected by their abilities to both engage with the dialectic between the prerequisites of the educational programme and use these prerequisites to support and enhance their own learning needs. Although Silen argued that the ability to take up an independent position seemed to be linked to metacognitive competencies related to an understanding of their own learning process, she did not delineate why some students were able to do this and others were not. Yet in Lahteenmaki's (2001) study, students did not raise this issue of self-direction but were concerned that they were not being guided step by step through the learning process. Lahteenmaki examined how students structured their learning in problem-based learning in their first year of studies in physiotherapy. She found that students were initially uncritical and enthusiastic, but later became concerned about whether they were learning enough material and whether they were learning the right pieces of knowledge. Although this appears to be a common concern for novice problem-based learning students, their later concerns reflect students' views about the kinds of learning expected within the discipline. It was particularly noticeable that students wanted to be given direction by the facilitator and wanted to be taught in an apprentice-style format, which reflects much of the way physiotherapy has been traditionally taught worldwide.

Preparing and equipping students for problem-based learning

Although the research into the way in which students are prepared for problem-based learning is sparse, this is a growing area of concern. Quantitative studies that have examined students' experiences of problem-based learning have shown that students are, in general, more satisfied with their experience of problem-based learning than other traditional lectured-based components of the programme (Warburton and Whitehouse 1998; Pau *et al.* 1999; Bligh *et al.* 2000). Hammel *et al.* (1999) and Liddle (2000) both explored students' experiences of a problem-based learning programme in occupational therapy using a participatory action research approach. The findings indicated that students perceived that when problem-based learning was adopted consistently across the programme, it contributed to their development of information management, critical reasoning, communication and team-building abilities. However, they also identified that students found time and role management challenging and the relationship between teaching and tutoring in problem-based learning ambiguous. This highlights that the shift for students in understanding the role of the facilitator is not only complex, but often made more difficult because the tutors are themselves in a state of transition, which often means that the students will be expected, normally covertly, to adapt with the tutor as they change their role over time. To date, there is little evidence about how the extent to which students are prepared affects their ability to adapt to problem-based learning readily. Some research has suggested that students' prior experiences of learning and their expectations of a problem-based programme do affect their adaptation to it over time (e.g. Ryan 1993; Savin-Baden 1996; Taylor 1997). Although there is a deficit in the literature on equipping students, many staff do prepare students for problem-based learning in a range of ways – from a one-hour introductory lecture to a two-week induction programme. King (2001) documented a week-long problem-based induction programme for students in medical radiation that included students undertaking adventure-based learning and experiential learning tasks.

Until recently in the UK, there was relatively little preparation of students for problem-based learning. Even in programmes that are over a third problem-based, many students receive little beyond a lecture on the rudiments of problem-based learning and a few team-building activities. This, however, is changing. Students are increasingly being asked to engage in problem-based learning seminars as part of their selection for the programme, although in some disciplines where under-recruitment is common, this is less likely to occur. Often in the first week of a module programme, they undertake a series of team activities, a problem scenario that does not relate to the discipline, which is designed to be both enjoyable and informative, and then periods of reflection and time for questions. There has also been a realization that students must no longer only be prepared for problem-based learning, but also the idea of being self-directed learners, as noted by Taylor (1997). To date, there is relatively little documentation of students' experiences of this.

The power of facilitation

Often when problem-based learning is implemented, there is a sense that this approach to learning will offer students freedom and independence in learning. Many of us have designed courses that enable students to meet the learning outcomes expected by benchmarking standards, the university and the professional body, yet have still managed to allow students a space to define and research their own needs as learners. Once this has been achieved, the challenges are two-fold. The first is that of being a facilitator who is aware of how they teach, why they teach that way and who has examined how their teaching is perceived by students. The second is to equip the students to take up the challenge of taking control of their own learning.

Yet just being aware of how we teach and the pedagogical stance we take up in relation to students is not enough. Barrett (2001) has argued that problem-based learning is a subset of problem-posing education. She draws on the work of Freire to suggest that it is only possible to know something through problematizing it. Freire (1972) asserted that knowledge acquisition must begin with problems, puzzles or tasks: 'In problem posing education, people develop their power to perceive critically the way they exist in the world with which they find themselves' (p. 70). Thus, she suggests, in problem-based learning the tutor facilitates a critical process whereby people are enabled to ask and answer questions. The work of Freire helps to delineate some important issues about power relations in problem-based learning and in particular the role of the facilitator. Specifically, Freire's view of power, oppression and liberation combines psychological, sociological and political perspectives. The result is that the process of personal development is one of managing the tension between oppression and liberation. From a Freirian perspective, social empowerment and growth in personal autonomy are not mutually exclusive but complementary. Thus for both the students and the facilitator, discussion about what counts as freedom, autonomy, self-direction and empowerment are vital to ensure that learning in teams is not an oppressive experience.

As I have noted earlier, and as Silen (2001) has argued, there remains little delineation or understanding about the notion of self-direction in problem-based learning, but there also seems to be little discussion about issues of power and control in this learning approach. Bernstein (1996) has suggested that power and control are embedded empirically within one another but that they are different. Power relations are seen as creating and legitimizing boundaries between categories and thus always operate to produce dislocations, whereas control establishes legitimate forms of communication appropriate to the different categories. Thus it would appear that induction into the discipline is a power mechanism, whereas the problematization of situations through empowering problem scenarios is a mechanism of control that allows for communication to be established both across disciplines and also between the theorizing of the discipline and the realities of practice. In the studies of Savin-Baden (1996, 2002), students' experiences of power and control appeared to relate strongly to the positioning of the facilitator within the team, yet facilitators' understandings of how they facilitated self-direction and devolved power to students seemed to be on a transitional continuum. Depending upon where staff positioned themselves on this continuum affected what occurred in the team and the expectation of who was in control. However, what is not evident from my own work or the recent research on staff and students' experiences of problem-based learning are the kinds of power issues at play in the teams and what the interrelationship between direction, covert control, manipulation, co-dependency and empowerment might be from the student perspective. Edwards (1997) has suggested that the exercise of power (as opposed to the notion of power relations Bernstein defined) can be seen as disciplinary and pastoral, which is a useful distinction in the context of problem-based learning. Disciplinary power is the process by which the State gains knowledge and understanding about the population to govern its people. Expert discourses about issues such as crime, madness and education are provided and, therefore, disciplinary knowledge becomes associated with particular practices and the induction into a particular kind of disciplinary identity. Thus in the problem-based community, academics will use disciplinary knowledge and power to guide (and also possibly) subjugate students into the discipline and encourage them to develop the appropriate disciplinary identity.

Pastoral power is exercised through the idea of confession that enables students to adjust their identity and desires to disciplinary regimes. The students buy into the notion of confession so that they become aligned through certain practices into the domain of power. Edwards (1997) has suggested that the significance of pastoral power can be seen in a range of approaches in education in which confession is central, such as portfolio-based assessment, continuous assessment and self-evaluation. Such practices encourage both staff and students to accept greater individual responsibility and this brings increased stress, but also 'pastoral power becomes self-replicating, creating the conditions for its own proliferation, as the form of "empowerment" engendered is the basis for the "problems" it seeks to resolve' (Edwards 1997: 10). There is a sense, then, that the proliferation of problem-based learning programmes could be seen as the exercising of pastoral power through the state via higher education, yet it is to be hoped that it is not such a sinister use of power that is emerging but instead it is the emergence of Freirian empowerment. However, the positioning of problem-based learning within the university and curriculum, the kinds of power exerted by the facilitator and what self-direction is taken to mean by the students will affect the way in which power, control, self-direction and empowerment are conceptualized and practised by staff and students involved in problem-based curricula.

Conclusion

Being an effective facilitator is more than just asking a particular type of open-ended question, adopting a body posture that speaks of interest and openness or providing a snug and cosy atmosphere. More is demanded of us than this. At its most basic level, the facilitator's position is one of being there to ensure that the team works effectively and that team members' learning needs are met. However, the facilitator is also there to promote the development of a team culture, to challenge, to help the balancing of task and process and to enable students to move from critical thinking to critical thought and then to critique. The position and type of power and understanding of students' perceptions and concerns are important components in what it means to be effective in the facilitation process. However, facilitation is also affected by notions of ethics and honesty in problem-based learning teams and it is to this that we turn next.

5

Facilitating Honesty in Problem-based Curricula

We still haven't solved the problem of students being committed to the problem-based learning group. Over the last three years we have tried everything: assessing the team and team-building activities. It is all very well for tutors at universities with really bright students, like the Ivy League and the Russell Group, where they are committed to learning for its own sake but it just won't work here.

You suggested that if we developed ground rules and used the tripartite assessment this might help our students to believe in the process of learning instead of concentrating on grades. Our medical students are highly motivated and are bright students so they don't see why other people should benefit from their work.

Our problem-based learning has been working well but we have had several instances of bullying in the problem-based learning teams over the last five years and we are not really sure what to do next. All the students who were bullied or marginalized in the problem-based learning teams have now left the course.

Although we have got students to work effectively in teams in several disciplines, the law students tend to collude with each other. The strategy is that they meet before the session where we use peer assessment and agree to give each other the same mark. We have tried to explain that there is mismatch with their behaviour and being lawyers, and argue that they need to take responsibility for being honest about how the team has really worked, but they don't take any notice.

Introduction

The cameos above represent many of the stories that are being told in the problem-based community about some of the ethical challenges that exist in the context of problem-based learning. Some tutors have suggested that the difficulties tend to be related to post-1992 universities and polytechnics, where students are not as committed to learning as those in the more traditional universities and the pre-1992 sector. Others have suggested that collusion is rife across all courses and disciplines because of the need to work to eat, and so students have little time to get involved in the process of learning. This chapter explores the underlying assumptions about students' views of learning through problem-based learning and examines the conceptions of ethics and honesty when working in learning teams. The final section of the chapter suggests ways of helping students to develop an ethical framework for working and learning through problem-based learning and of assisting staff to design problem-based curricula in ways that discourage unethical behaviour.

Honest teamwork?

One of the central principles of problem-based learning is that students work and learn in teams. The size of the team varies depending on the discipline, cohort and university, but the general trend in the UK is to utilize teams of between 8 and 12 students. Throughout the literature on problem-based learning, there is little on students working in groups or teams. Learning groups gained popularity in higher education in the 1960s, a trend that has continued. Teams are often equated with games, such as football and basketball, where the members have different roles but equal status. For many years, the word 'team' has also been used in commerce and industry to denote a group of people engaged in a specific task with a clear remit, but who make decisions together. Yet in higher and professional education, this term appears to be used little, the more loosely bounded expression of 'group' being preferred. The problem here is that to talk of problem-based learning groups implies that a cluster of people have come together with a collective perception, with shared aims and having made the choice to work and learn together. Often this is not the case, since students have been allocated to groups and the task is invariably predetermined. In addition, some students only undertake problem-based learning because it is a condition of their choice of course or subject.

Groups are often places where joining is part of the process of becoming cohesive, where there is a sense that people choose to be present and that they have an option to leave at any time. Teams differ in that they demand a different kind of ethos, culture and commitment. To belong to a team usually means that there is a common purpose, a limited membership and that the team has the power to make decisions. Teams have a focus, a set of team rules and are time-limited. Thus a team is organized to meet together; it has a context and a task. As such, it would appear that the term 'team' is more appropriate for what occurs in most problem-based learning seminars because there is a focus, a remit and much of the learning that occurs evolves through the ways in which the team members make decisions about what and how they learn. However, before we explore issues connected with the working of the team, it is first important to explore what it is that individuals bring to the team and the ways in which their roles, behaviours and perspectives on team learning can impact upon the team as a whole. Building teams in the first instance will help the members to develop a sense of commitment that will sustain it through demanding periods of growth and development. Yet in our fragmented and incoherent society, there are difficulties with commitment and teamwork. Discussions in the press and over dinner at conferences often centre on what it means to be a student at university – for example, are they there to read for a degree? Does supplying handouts to facilitate learning constitute the promotion of a dependency culture in higher education? In problem-based learning, the questions about what counts as attendance and how students can be encouraged to be committed to the team, but also be autonomous learners, is still hotly debated.

One way of helping students to understand how they are operating within a problem-based learning team is to encourage them to explore their interactional stance. Interactional stance captures the way in which a learner interacts with others within a learning situation. It refers to the relationships between students within teams and staff–student relationships at both an individual and a team level. Thus interactional stance encompasses the way in which students interpret the way they as individuals, and others with whom they learn, construct meaning in relation to one another. Interactional stance has four domains which are dealt with in detail elsewhere (Savin-Baden 2000a), and summarized here.

The ethic of individualism

This reflects the way in which some students see learning within the team as an activity that is only valuable in terms of what they as an individual can gain from it. Such students place little value upon collective learning experiences and are more concerned that they may forego marks by expending effort-sharing tasks and information within the team rather than if they worked alone. This domain is characterized by the individual placing himself at the centre of the value system and, therefore, learning within the team is an activity that is only valuable in terms of personal gain for the individual.

Validated knowing through real talk

Real talk requires careful listening; it implies a mutually shared agreement that together you are creating the optimum setting so that half-baked ideas can grow. The domain of validated knowing captures the idea that through the experience of being heard within a team, and being valued by other team members, individual students learn to value their own knowledge and experience. Prior experiences of the individual are valued as a resource for learning by other team members and simultaneously prior experiences begin to be valued, sometimes for the first time, by the individuals. For students in this domain, learning in teams is often accompanied by a boost of self-esteem and confidence and, as a consequence, a renewed exploration and facilitation of individual learning aspirations. Being in this domain enables students to come to value their personal and propositional knowledge by recognizing its value through the perspectives of others.

Connecting experience through interaction

This domain is characterized by the individual being facilitated through the team process in making sense, through reflection, of his own reality and in confronting dilemmas and problems within that reality. For example, through role-play or discussion within a team, students may be helped to make sense of previous situations, experiences or issues that they had not previously understood. Through interpretation of information about himself and his experiences, obtained from other team members, the individual would learn to develop self-knowledge. Thus in this domain students use the team to both *make sense* of their world *as it appears to be* and to resolve dilemmas and discover meaning in their lives.

Transactional dialogue: mediating different worlds

Transactional dialogue (after Brookfield 1985) is used here to capture the idea that the team serves as an interactive function for the individual. Through the team, the individual is enabled to learn both through the experience of others and the appreciation of other people's life-worlds and, by reflecting upon these, to relate them to their own. Thus individual students, by making themselves and their learning the focus of reflection and analysis within the team, are able to value alternative ways of knowing. Dialogue here is central to progress in people's lives and it is through dialogue that values are deconstructed and reconstructed, and experiences relived and explored, to make sense of roles and relationships. This domain is concerned with identity building through the team process, so that students use the team process to challenge identity and all that is implicit within that identity.

Many problems associated with teams and the facilitator's role seem to be located within the larger context of unease associated with self-directed learning programmes. Differing understandings of self-direction appear to cause confusion and disjunction for staff, students, practitioners, professional bodies and institutions. In this sense the teams, and the facilitator role within these teams, could be seen as a microcosm of broader issues relating to the implementation and integration of problem-based learning within professional courses in higher education. Thus the domain students take up may reflect not just their own perspectives and motivations, but also their view about the purpose of the team and the extent to which the team and the facilitator prompt and enhance effective team learning. For teams to work effectively, it is important that students are clear not only about their individual role and perspectives in the team, but also the aims and goals of the team as a whole. It is only through such understanding that effective team motivation and commitment can be achieved.

Teamwork or plagiarism

The shifts towards self-directed learning, autonomous learning and particularly the perception of students as consumers seems to be promoting a notion of individualism that signals an end to dialogue and with it a devaluing of collaborative and dialogic approaches to learning. One of the growing challenges when adopting problem-based learning is promoting effective collaborative learning while also ensuring that plagiarism does not occur. Today, plagiarism is big business. Not only are there websites that supply essays for a fee, there are also those where students can cut and paste large components of materials into their essays at no expense. Although there is a growing literature and numerous websites on plagiarism, there has been little examination of it in the context of problem-based learning. However, before we consider problem-based learning and plagiarism, it is first important to understand what is meant by plagiarism and other related terms.

Plagiarism is considered to be the passing off of work done by someone else, intentionally or unintentionally, as your own, for your own benefit (Carroll 2002). The difficulty with plagiarism is that there are degrees of plagiarism and this, to some extent, overlaps with collusion and cheating. What is important to understand about plagiarism is that the passing off of work by someone else is related to giving a false impression, or of fooling or tricking. Although this could be seen to be deliberate dishonesty, plagiarism is also difficult territory because whether the tricking was intentional or unintentional, it is still classed as plagiarism. Yet at the same time there is often an assumption that plagiarism is about the use or borrowing of words when in fact it is about 'work' done rather than just the borrowing of words. However, if plagiarism is mentioned in a staff common room, invariably two mistaken assumptions are made. The first is that plagiarism has necessarily been intentional fraud, whereas much research has indicated that very little of it is fraud and much more of it is related to students' misunderstanding of both the assessment task and plagiarism itself (Franklyn-Stokes and Newstead 1995; Chester 2001). The second assumption is that most plagiarism is web-based, when in fact it is actually print-based. Although there are several websites where students can download essays and just adapt them to their own needs, when one examines such sites it is possible to see that a considerable amount is required of students. Adapting their essay demands changing words, adding references and adapting paragraphs, and it is evident that it would often take them just as long to adapt the plagiarized essay and add in the new relevant references than it would be to write the essay themselves in the first place. Many students plagiarize because they have not planned enough time for the work and thus it is commonly done at the last minute. The reasons students have given for plagiarism include poor time management (e.g. too many assignments and deadlines), poor judgement about time management (e.g. managing home and work commitments) and not understanding what is required of them. Not understanding includes an assumption that the assignment is beyond their capability, or finding that the requirements of the assignment are unclear or misunderstanding about what counts as academic writing.

Preventing plagiarism in problem-based learning

Recent research and literature on plagiarism suggest several ways of dealing with it, which include getting students to be involved in active teaching methods that demand that they express their opinions and take a view on issues about which they are reading. Other suggestions include getting students to create annotated bibliographies and using teaching approaches that require that they paraphrase and summarize books and articles (Carroll 2002). Problem-based learning is an approach to learning that encourages such capabilities in students but, at the same time, other difficulties related to plagiarism emerge, in particular the relationship between plagiarism, collusion and cheating in the context of teamwork. The difficulties here stem from a number of misunderstandings commonly heard in problem-based learning teams, some of which were exemplified in the cameos at the beginning of the chapter. Not all of these examples would appear, at first glance, to be about plagiarism, but they may lead to plagiarism or cheating by some or all of the team.

Collaboration, collusion or plagiarism?

An anecdote told recently of a student's complaint when they were found to have plagiarized was 'this is not fair, the student I copied from didn't tell me he had copied it'. In problem-based learning, it is expected that students will work and learn collaboratively, although it is not always made clear what counts as collaboration and how collusion might be defined. Collaboration is seen as working together in some form of intellectual activity, whereas collusion is more usually associated with copying work from a fellow student. What has not been addressed in the problem-based learning community is the point at which collaboration becomes collusion. In problem-based learning teams, students are expected to share researched information, personal knowledge and experience and are expected to debate issues. However, students need to understand that common knowledge can be defined as facts that are known generally or known by many people. Yet if a student submits jointly written course work as an individual piece of work or agrees to share the same mark in inter- or intra-peer assessment, this would be classed as collusion. Many students do not realize that not contributing equitably to group work where the work is submitted for a group mark is actually plagiarism. During the process of working with staff and students in research and consultancy, both have complained about students not contributing to the team and subsequently benefiting significantly from the work of others, yet this has never been seen as plagiarism. Students need to understand what counts as plagiarism and staff need to take steps to ensure both they and students understand the difference between collaboration, collusion and plagiarism.

Commitment to the team

Ensuring that students are committed to the team is a common problem and one that is usually best managed initially through building the team effectively in the first instance. Many staff implement problem-based learning but fail to provide sufficient time to build the team. The argument is often that there is not time within the curriculum, yet I would suggest that not assigning time for team building costs more time at a later stage of the course. Cormack (1989) has suggested that low commitment to the team will mean that decisions made by the team will not be implemented and that the quality and quantity of work will be low. This will result in little satisfaction and relationships within the team will deteriorate. Cormack has suggested that improving team commitment demands a positive approach by creating visions within the team, offering positive feedback and changing team roles to promote growth within the membership. A particularly useful strategy Cormack proposes is that of the facilitator talking with each team member about their concerns and asking them what they think needs to be done. In problem-based learning teams, this will encourage students to take responsibility for difficulties within the team and help them to consider ways of progressing.

However, it is not only important to ensure students are committed but that they are also equipped to deal with conflict, and that they understand their responsibility in conflict management in relation to each other and the facilitator. As a novice facilitator, I was working with a newly formed problem-based learning team and, when it broke down, I just asked them to sort out the conflict themselves, emphasizing in particular that their learning was their responsibility. Admittedly this was pushing the notion of students' autonomy and self-direction a little far, but it does raise several concerns about conflict management, lines of responsibility and particular ways of facilitating effective teams.

Effective teamwork

Much of what has been written in the literature about effective teams centres on the achievement of goals, the need for clear team roles and sound team leadership. However, in problem-based learning teams, effectiveness is not about goals and roles but instead about learning and collaboration. Effectiveness then demands that the team values the capabilities and knowledge of its members and ensures that authority is shared. There seems to be an assumption in many undergraduate problem-based learning programmes that if teams appear to be content, then they are necessarily effective. This may reflect facilitators' anxiety about ensuring students, as consumers, are satisfied with the course or that the facilitators are concerned about their own roles and responsibilities as teachers. Whether a team is effective or not depends largely on what is expected of the students in the team by those who designed the programme, the facilitator, and the students themselves. Nevertheless, I would argue that commitment and effectiveness in teamwork are interrelated and are affected by the way in which the team manages the different tasks and processes in which it is involved. Heron (1993) proposed that teams engage in four types of task:

- *Renewal tasks*: such tasks involve using or updating equipment or undertaking education and training. Teams involved in such tasks include technical teams and staff development teams.
- *Development tasks*: here the work of the team is to innovate and work in new directions and often to solve or manage problems. A problem-based learning team would be one that is, in general, focused on development tasks.
- *Production tasks*: the team's function here is to produce goods or services.
- *Crisis tasks*: the team role is to deal with dangers, emergencies and critical events. Some problem-based learning teams (in areas such as health, social care and disaster management) may be involved in this area.

Heron has suggested that too much focus on one of these areas results in distortions within the team. Problems then emerge in the forms of teams becoming person-bound, problem-bound, role-bound or power-bound. His notion of teams becoming problem-bound is particularly useful in the context of problem-based learning. Teams preoccupied with problem-solving work tend to become focused on goals, planning and achievement:

> This means that decision-making control becomes subservient to a preoccupation with problem-solving tasks and the pursuit of technical know-how, and this is at the expense of a coherent social structure, and of personnel welfare.
>
> (Heron 1993: 125)

The result is that in problem-based learning teams, there is a tendency to try to solve or manage the problem scenario at all times and at all costs, rather than focusing on wider team issues and investing in long-term team goals that will build the team up. Thus interpersonal concerns often become distorted or lost.

Improving assessment through understanding plagiarism

Although assessment will be dealt with in detail in Chapter 8, ways of preventing plagiarism will be outlined here. There are currently a number of electronic sites that check work for cheating, copying and plagiarism, but it is preferable to develop forms of assessment that prevent it occurring in the first place. Before students hand in their work, there are some procedures that can be in place to help to lessen the possibility of plagiarism, which include:

1. *Assessing both the process and product of teamwork.* Often in problem-based teams there will be some students who do little work and expect to be carried along by the rest of the team. For such students, the collaborative nature of teamwork means that team effort can be exploited. The use of assessments that require students to produce their reflections on the team progress and process, synchronous and asynchronous online discussion and reflective journals can all be ways of preventing collusion.
2. *Reconsider how assessments are used.* Many programmes still retain essays but the traditional essay is easy to plagiarize. Ways of avoiding this include not

only using case-based or scenario-based essays, but also using different kinds of assessment that demand that students utilize knowledge in different ways. For example, by using assessments that expect students to develop a strategy and then substantiating it or engaging with moral dilemma will not only promote critical thought but also prevent plagiarism. Other types of assessment that could be used are an outline of an essay with sources and resources that could be used, critical incident analyses or an annotated bibliography.

3. *Additional strategies.* Many of the assessments currently in use are ambiguous in the use of terminology and this confuses students (for example, what is the difference between critically evaluates and evaluates?) Ensuring the essay title and instructions are clear and understandable will help students to know what is expected and encourage them to do the work themselves. However, asking for drafts of work, particularly project work, can ensure the students are the authors and in research projects and dissertations, field diaries and audio tapes can be submitted as proof of authenticity.

Increasingly, students are being asked to sign statements of originality in which they assert that the work is their own and is as a result of their own effort. In the context of problem-based learning, a strategy that is also being used when work is collaborative is that the components of the work are ascribed to the individuals involved. This not only helps to prevent plagiarism but also promotes equity and responsibility within the team.

Towards an ethical framework for problem-based learning

To date there has been limited discussion in the literature about the notion of ethics in problem-based learning and relatively little in the literature on group work; however, the subject of values is discussed in the context of group facilitation and arenas such as action learning. Values in general relate to our belief systems and, although in teams it is possible to have shared values, the real difficulty is that we do not always operate in ways that we have espoused. In higher education, both staff and students tend to assume that the learning community is one that is caring and supportive of its learners, but in recent years it has become a place of competition, with poor communication and sometimes abusive styles of management. As we have seen in the cameos, there are a number of difficulties for students in problem-based teams and these are inflated by the acceptable deception in the media, politics, professional practice and higher education in general. Both higher educational and professional practice are littered with outcome measures, evidence-based practice and trite quantitative practices that do little justice to students and their lives. This audit culture has led to a minefield of unintended consequences and has become a machine for dishonesty. Collusion and dishonesty are not just part of the world of research, but also the world of learning and teaching: 'professional culture has institutionalized universalistic standards of service delivery, regardless of the personal characteristics of the client which are irrelevant to the professional relationship' (Turner 1993: 14).

Many of the texts on groups and teamwork have argued that team members should help to develop conditions where each member can negotiate, cooperate and fulfil their own needs. In the context of problem-based learning, two principles in particular can help teams to develop such conditions. First, exploring the principle of autonomy means that students have freedom to choose, take decisions and then be accountable for such decisions. This principle also means that facilitators must honour the right of the students to make choices about what they do and do not do in the team, and be able to make an informed choice about activities in which they will be expected to engage. Such a principle is a good one, but in the context of higher education and current models of problem-based learning this is difficult to implement. Part of the challenge here is because of the second principle, that of informed consent. There are several difficulties with informed consent. For example, different types of consent have different implications for the team and the curriculum as a whole. Much of the consent that occurs in teaching and particularly problem-based learning is tacit consent, agreement through not objecting or implied consent which is inferred from actions. Thus commitment to the team and what staff and students mean by commitment is complex and often remains uncontested by students. The result is that sometimes students fall short of commitment to the team, but the conflict that often ensues is invariably ignored and not dealt with by the team or the facilitator.

The challenge for many problem-based facilitators is to encourage and sustain the principles of autonomy and informed consent in the context of assessment, competition and demanding workloads. It is often the case that difficulties in relationships between students and facilitator and among team members themselves are caused to some extent by having an implicit understanding of trust and non-concealment. Trust in teams is fragile and something that needs to be built, maintained and sustained. Honesty in teams is often difficult with high workloads, endless assessment deadlines often caused by modularization, and the temptation to plagiarize. Thus ethical questions do not rest purely around the issues about how to behave – ethics have to be understood in terms of the relationships made with those in the team. This can be particularly difficult for facilitators, since they can be in a position where their obligations as a facilitator conflict with those as a teacher in higher education. Heron (1993) suggested that facilitator authority is paradoxical because of the way in which the facilitator has to pass on to the students some body of knowledge and skill through a process of learning that promotes and affirms the autonomy of the learner. What Heron is suggesting is that facilitators are not only intellectually competent in relation to their subject area, but also bring interpersonal, emotional and political capabilities, so that their holistic grasp of their subject helps students to develop interconnection between themselves and the subject. Examples that might help students include the following

Recognize and engage with students' interactional stances within the team

Students need to be encouraged to explore their role and stance within the team. Although it is possible to use diagnostic tools such as Belbin's (1993) team roles to help students to understand their roles in teams, these often do not acknowledge the interplay of students' perceptions of knowledge, learning and autonomy in relation to how they see themselves as learners within the team. Recognizing their interactional stance, and possibly also examining their pedagogical stance, will help students to understand how they interact with others within a learning environment and enable them to examine the relationships between students within their team and staff–student relationships at both an individual and a team level.

Help students to understand and discuss plagiarism

Few students understand what counts as plagiarism. Therefore, activities should be undertaken within the team to help students to understand what it is. In particular, they need to examine the differences between plagiarism, collusion and collaboration. A useful starting point might be to ask them as a team to explore the assessments on the course and find ways that they can plagiarize or collude. Having understood the differences between plagiarism, collusion and collaboration, the team can then be encouraged to contract with each other to collaborate rather than collude so that they all become stakeholders in both the agreement and the assessment.

Understand sources and effects of conflict on individuals and teams

Conflict often emerges when one person wants what they cannot have (Cormack 1989). This straightforward definition contains much of value, but conflict in teams is generally more complicated than this. Team conflict tends to relate to issues of power and personality, which can be seen in the way in which team members manage the border between their stances within the team and the territories that they believe belong to them within a team. What occurs in many higher education programmes is a form of bullying where one student ridicules another or criticizes them openly. Bullying has occurred in higher education, but it tends to be more apparent in problem-based teams because of the demands and the intensity of teamwork. Team conflict in problem-based learning often results in a member being marginalized or dominated by another and because staff and students are often not equipped or prepared to deal with conflict the impact can be colossal on the individual. Students have spoken of being frightened to attend their team, of leaving in tears or of developing a psychosomatic illness because of the stress of learning in a team. There is a large literature on conflict management and developing trigger materials to help students to engage with this, and the literature on bullying is an important means of discussing and helping students to manage conflict at the start of the course.

Realize facilitator responsibility within the team

Being a responsible facilitator is a topic that is still debated with a great deal of heat and tension. Much of what is executed depends upon the subject area or discipline, but the following points may help some staff to consider what might count as responsibility with the team:

- help students to understand informed consent;
- create a forum for students to discuss ethics in teamwork;
- discuss the role and responsibility of the facilitator in the team and present research that shows facilitator and student development changes depending on the context and the experience of both;
- design materials to prevent plagiarism and change these regularly;
- use assessment that prevents plagiarism.

Develop ethical behaviour

Honesty is not just about work that is submitted for assessment, it is also about ethical behaviour within teams. In action learning, many of the values related to this approach to learning reflect the voluntary nature of set membership. Voluntarily joining and remaining a member of an action learning set is founded on the values held by the set (McGill and Beaty 2001). Yet few problem-based learning teams, particularly in undergraduate education, are voluntary; rather, problem-based teamwork is a condition of the course. This kind of conditional membership means that values about joining and being committed do not apply to problem-based learning teams in the same way as action learning sets. It may be possible to develop codes or principles to which students comply, but it must be recognized that such codes cannot govern behaviour but only help to guide it. For example, the principles of autonomy, non-maleficence, beneficence and informed consent could be sound starting points for helping a team to develop an ethical framework in which to learn.

Conclusion

One of the main difficulties with plagiarism is that students do not understand what it is. Many do not realize that what they are doing could be counted as plagiarism, collusion or cheating; therefore, until they do, it is difficult to manage. Although there are several texts and papers that document ways of countering plagiarism, it is important that it is dealt with early on problem-based learning teams so that it does not become a significant problem and result in team breakdown. Further debate is needed in the problem-based community about ways in which we can ensure that work presented by students and teams is trustworthy and authentic. Students should be encouraged to show how the work presented as a piece under-taken by the team has evolved and where there has been disagreement and negotiation. There also needs to be greater overt discussion in the team about the nature of consent and responsibility. It is also important that ways are found of ensuring that debates occur about what counts as ethical behaviour and strategies are devised to ensure equity, honesty and fairness are central principles in problem-based learning teams.

Part 3

Facilitation: Changing Worlds

6

Developing and Supporting Facilitators

Introduction

Based on the literature and my own experience, this chapter argues that there is limited research into the process and management of problem-based learning staff development. The current shift towards problem-based learning within higher education suggests that staff and educational development needs to be a central component in any problem-based learning implementation strategy. The chapter deals with ways of providing staff development in relation to problem-based learning. Suggestions are made about ways of executing staff and educational development programmes and providing mechanisms for continuing support for staff as they implement problem-based learning.

Cash for control?

In recent years in the UK, there has been a shift towards improving teaching in higher education. What this has meant in practice is that large sums of money have been allocated to institutions that have demonstrated and implemented a learning and teaching strategy. The effect has been a wide-scale focus on learning and teaching in universities in the UK, rather than just research, and this has produced some interesting consequences. In 1998, the Higher Education Funding Council for England (HEFCE) commissioned research into the use of learning and teaching strategies in English institutions. This was undertaken in the context of a shift towards more centralized and strategic management of change than previously. The background to this reform was predominantly in response to external forms of assessment, such as the Research Assessment Exercise and Teaching Quality Assessment (Gibbs *et al.* 2000). Furthermore, the MacFarlane Report (Committee of Scottish University Principles 1992) had argued for a strong link between the institutional learning and teaching strategy and the institutional plan. Cost-cutting, modularization, innovation, new and different teaching methods and roles, all contributed to an increased need for greater planning. Lecturers no longer had the time or resources to manage such complex change. What was interesting about the survey commissioned by HEFCE (undertaken by Gibbs *et al.* 2000) was the emergence and rapid development of learning and teaching strategies in institutions and the way such development has both promoted change and guided policy. In the study, 63 institutions submitted information to support their claim to have a learning and teaching strategy, 62 reported that such a strategy was under development and submitted various draft documentation and four said that they did not have one, nor were they developing one. Gibbs *et al.* highlighted the fact that the development of such a strategy was a recent phenomenon, the earliest being dated 1990, and that while many remained unchanged five years later, others had developed resource centres, task groups and senior management positions for the promotion of learning and teaching. Yet they argued that many institutions have not operationalized their values and goals and have stopped short of action planning (Gibbs *et al.* 2000). Thus at an institutional level there appears to be plenty of learning and teaching strategies, many of which mention problem-based learning, but as yet there is little understanding of the purpose of such strategies or how they might be implemented or sustained.

At the same time, what has occurred wholesale across the UK has been the professionalization of teaching. Staff in most UK universities are expected to have a teaching qualification – even if many still do not have one – and staff new to the university system are required to attend a mandatory programme in learning and teaching usually provided by the in-university educational development unit. The consequences of this have not only been the elevation of the status of teaching and such development units, but also forms of innovative learning that are seen to promote particular capabilities in students, such as e-learning, autonomous learning and problem-based learning. However, a number of difficulties have emerged through this new money and new focus on teaching. The first is the positioning of educational development in universities, the second is the implementation of learning and teaching strategies and the third is the place of pedagogic research in universities.

Positioning educational development in universities

Since the growth of educational development units in universities in the 1970s, there has always been controversy about their role and place within the university. Many people involved in educational development would suggest that the popularity of such units within a given university changes on a five-year cycle and this can be seen in the way such units are placed both physically and metaphorically within the university. Many educational development units have sought to be independent from faculties, particularly education faculties, and for most this has been both a source of strength and of weakness. What has been interesting with the new focus on teaching in universities has been the increased status of such units. They have become the producers and implementers of programmes to teach staff how to teach effectively and the reason that many universities have secured large sums of money for teaching. Take, for example, the post-1992 universities, which already valued teaching highly and were able to bid for large sums of money to support current practices and develop new ones. While this is both valuable and commendable, there appears to be a lack of criticality in many of the programmes for staff, whereby new staff are inducted into a language of professional learning and particular kinds of teaching and learning techniques. For example, there is often unquestioning adoption of the notion of deep and surface approaches to learning, reflective practice and learning styles, with little recourse to the current literature that contests such work. For example, Barnett (1997) has argued for more complex undertakings of reflection to be taken up and Haggis (2002) suggests the continued adherence to deep and surface approaches to learning is misplaced. This is not the case in every university, but it appears to be a trend. The difficulty with this kind of professionalization of learning is that issues of self identity and context are largely ignored, when in fact these vital components need to be explored in depth when introducing staff to learning practices, such as problem-based learning, that demand a recognition of the stances of both learners and teachers in the learning context.

Managing pedagogic change in universities

Amidst the procurement of money to improve teaching, the appointment of teaching fellows and the elite national teaching awards, there appears to be some curious assumptions being made. The first is that organizational change and innovation in teaching can be managed in curricula and in universities in such a way and that such change would have an impact over time. While such initiatives are laudable, there has been little real questioning of what the long-term impact and sustainability of such initiatives might be. It may be that universities can reward staff for good teaching through promotion to a chair, but in reality this may have relatively little impact on the teaching that occurs in the university on undergraduate courses in general. What is needed instead is a learning and teaching strategy underpinned by sound educational principles. Such a strategy should draw on recent pedagogic research which has goals that are achievable and has impact across the whole university and which is overseen by a senior manager who can take a critical stance on what is being attempted. This would then mean that new initiatives, such as problem-based learning, are centred within the broader university learning and teaching strategy, rather than the current practice where there is a tendency to decide to implement problem-based learning and then a few staff just doing so. Locating innovations in teaching in the wider political context of universities will mean that the position of learning, teaching and assessment in the curriculum, along with the role and position of educational development, will enable shifts to be made about understandings of knowledge and knowledge creation. Such relocation will also encourage staff and students to contest the views of knowledge and the values surrounding the kinds of knowledge that are seen as paramount in the discipline and in the wider university system.

Learning and teaching strategies

The inclusion of problem-based learning in many university learning and teaching strategy documents at one level is encouraging because of the realization of its importance in promoting independent inquiry. However, at another level it is also of concern. The concern is not about the decision to use problem-based learning *per se*, but rather the sub-text of such ideas, which seem to point up difficulties in understandings about what a learning and teaching strategy is perceived to be, what it is for and thus how such a strategy is to be implemented. The evidence (Gibbs *et al.* 2000) suggests that few university managers understood what their strategy was and often it was seen to be a document that spoke of ways of teaching – such as problem-based learning, e-learning and lectures – rather than an explanation of the kinds of learning and teaching intentions and goals for the university over the subsequent five years.

The increased use of problem-based learning has brought with it a great demand for staff and educational development. In some disciplines and countries, the focus is on staff development; in others, it is on educational development. Staff development in general tends to focus upon equipping staff with skills to implement problem-based learning through training workshops that offer hints and tips. In practice, what often occurs is that a particular disciplinary area will have its curriculum revalidated with the magical words 'problem-based learning' inserted into the curriculum document somewhere that seemed appropriate, and then the mechanics of how this is going to be implemented is thought about afterwards. Soon after validation it is realized that implementing the problem-based learning component is perhaps a little more difficult than was first thought and so a training consultant is found to help with the implementation. In these circumstances, staff development comprises a series of training days on given topics such as trigger development, assessment, small group learning and how to use problem-based learning in large groups. So rather than problem-based learning being seen as a core component of the curriculum, it is added on and attempts are made to knit it in with the rest of the (often didactic) curriculum. These training days may be well run and very helpful in equipping staff in starting to use problem-based learning, but in many cases they do not get to the heart of challenges. For example, I was at a conference a few years ago where alongside the usual keynotes and presentations were a series of workshops on various topics related to problem-based learning. The idea was that the workshops would help you to implement problem-based learning or to improve what you were doing. The workshops were helpful and instructive but predominantly led by the experts who tended to talk for half the session and then encourage some discussion in small groups for the remainder of the session. The difficulty here, and with staff development programmes that are essentially 'how to' training sessions, is that they begin from the assumption that participants need particular kinds of skills or information that can be bolted on to the curriculum. Problem-based learning was being treated as if it were just another teaching technique, that with a few hints and tips could simply be applied categorically across all subjects and disciplines, with little thought being given to the discipline itself or to the constructivist nature of problem-based learning.

Staff development that comprises training in techniques is not needed; what is required instead is educational development. What I mean is that instead of receiving training, staff are encouraged to review their position in an educational way. In practice, the workshop would not contain hints and tips, but instead would engage staff with problem-based learning by first exploring the concept of the curriculum and the place of problem-based learning within it. This approach helps staff not only to examine their assumptions about what might count as a curriculum, but also helps them to explore their understanding about learning and knowledge, and their views about autonomy.

To date, relatively little has been written about educational development for problem-based learning. There are widely held views about the kinds of development that should be undertaken to equip, develop and support staff in becoming facilitators. Yet the area of staff development is perceived to be key to the success of problem-based learning (Nayer 1995). This is demonstrated by the number of staff development workshops documented in recent years (e.g. Almy *et al.* 1992; Holmes and Kaufman 1994; Little 1997; Wilkerson and Hundert 1997). However, few studies have documented the processes and outcomes of staff development and progress, or have evaluated the success of staff training or indeed staff perspectives.

The role, satisfaction, effectiveness and training of staff in problem-based learning programmes is still under-researched and literature that is currently available in general often documents accounts of staff development programmes (e.g. Del Mar 1997; Kippers *et al.* 1997; Rayan 1997). What has tended to happen is that general principles of staff and educational development have been adapted to equip staff for problem-based learning by consultants who, while well versed in educational development, have not always implemented problem-based learning or designed a problem-based curriculum. Alternatively, staff wanting to implement problem-based learning read a considerable amount of literature and then attend a generic staff development workshop on problem-based learning at one of the centres of excellence, such as the University of Maastricht in the Netherlands, the University of Delaware in the USA or McMaster University in Canada. All of these strategies may equip staff to implement problem-based learning, but there are a number of difficulties with them. The first is that while using generic staff development consultants to help with the implementation of problem-based learning may be helpful, if they have not used problem-based learning themselves they are not always aware of some of the stumbling blocks that staff experience, or some of the common mistakes that can be made when designing problem-based curricula. Attending three-day workshops at one of the centres of excellence, while being informative, is invariably not sensitive to cultural or disciplinary differences. This can leave staff with the view that they have to do it the 'McMaster way' or adopt 'the seven-stage model' used by Maastricht, instead of developing a model that will suit their university and disciplinary culture and fit with the needs of their programme. Thus, to implement problem-based learning in a way that promotes sound educational development, it is important to plan the introduction of it into the curriculum some two years before the whole curriculum is changed to problem-based learning. This will allow sufficient time to decide on the kind of programme that is to be designed and to prepare staff adequately for the introduction of this new approach. Many staff wanting to introduce problem-based learning begin by making a few modules problem-based and then, having become used to the approach, spend time redesigning the curriculum as a whole. This incremental approach works effectively and also helps staff to adjust over a period of time. However, it is also important to make the distinction between initial and on-going educational development.

Initial educational development

The principles of initial educational development stem from the need for staff to begin the shift towards problem-based learning by examining their own pedagogical stances and perspectives on the curriculum. This kind of activity needs, ideally, to be undertaken with colleagues in the same institution and subject area, so that realistic discussion can be had about what is possible within the given university structure. For example, a starting point may be to use a problem-based learning consultant to run a one-day workshop within a university to help staff to examine the ways it might be implemented. Thereafter, it is often advisable to have series of workshops that focus on a discipline or on areas that have shared disciplines, such as the allied health professions or engineering and physics. Having spoken to a number of colleagues, experience would suggest that a three-day workshop is advisable. Such a workshop can be undertaken over three consecutive days or one day a week for three weeks. There should be no more than twenty participants and staff should be committed to attending all three days. This is because spending time as a group working through the issues helps staff to grapple with them in depth, and staff subsequently become much clearer about the issues relating to the implementation of problem-based learning. A three-day period also helps staff to deal with any disjunction they have regarding problem-based learning and gives them the opportunity to share their concerns. In the current climate of higher education, in which student numbers are high and staff time is very limited for learning about new approaches, it could be argued that this is a very expensive form of educational development. However, programmes where problem-based learning have been implemented successfully and have been maintained over time invariably have been the ones that have put time and funding into equipping staff to implement it from the outset. A suggested schedule for implementation is outlined in Table 6.1.

The schedule in Table 6.1 allows for the practising of problem-based learning, with some initial educational development in the first two years for facilitators, which will then support them through the first year of implementation. In year 3, the whole curriculum is changed to problem-based learning and on-going support by an external consultant allows for readjustments to be made and facilitators to be supported through the change process. The inclusion of student preparation at the beginning of the first year when problem-based learning is to be used is vital, so that the students understand the process. On-going commitment to student preparation and support is also essential, so that they are helped to adjust to

Table 6.1   Suggested schedule for the introduction of problem-based learning over a whole curriculum

---

Year 1

Three-day educational development workshops provided for all staff

Optional extra workshop days provided with external consultant for development of trigger materials and redesign of assessments to fit with learning approach

Trigger materials designed for introduction into two modules

Year 2

Problem-based learning introduced into one or two modules

Students' on-going evaluation of problem-based learning modules introduced: results to inform new curriculum

Process of curriculum redesign commenced with focus on the content that staff want students to learn

Meetings convened with professional body/colleagues to discuss planned changes

Year 3

Learning intentions translated into curriculum levels with appropriate problem-based assessment

Learning opportunities designed: problem-based learning seminars, lectures, skills sessions, fieldwork

Three-day educational development workshops provided for staff who missed first workshop or have recently joined university

Year 4

Curriculum revalidated

Two-week problem-based learning induction programme provided for first students

Monthly facilitator support group help with external consultant

Year 5

Master classes commenced

Trigger material evaluated

New trigger materials developed

Three-day educational development workshops provided for staff who have recently joined university

---

problem-based learning. The incorporation of an ongoing evaluation means that the findings of the evaluation can be used to make changes in the curriculum as it progresses. A more detailed example of initial preparation of facilitators is presented in Murray and Savin-Baden (2000). The recommendations for educational development of staff include :

- The preparation for facilitators needs to start as early as possible, at least one year ahead of the start of the programme in which problem-based learning is to be used.
- The development of trigger materials should involve all groups of staff contributing to the delivery of a particular module.

- The production of learning resources is vital to the success of problem-based learning and related departments need to be involved from the outset.
- Faculty educational development needs to be paralleled with the introduction of problem-based learning into the clinical/practice environment.
- Faculty support is vital in enhancing the likelihood of success of introducing problem-based learning into the curriculum.
- In-depth discussion of assessment methods should be a key component of any staff development programme.

On-going educational development

It is often the case that once a three-day programme of educational development has been undertaken, staff are then expected to implement the curriculum with little on-going support. Yet for many staff, the implementation of the programme and support while they become familiar with the approach are as important as the initial workshops. Recent research (Savin-Baden 2002; Wilkie 2002) has shown that staff roles as facilitators evolve over time and that many require support as they make the shift away from more didactic approaches, characterized by giving clear directions to students about what and how to learn and providing short talks in the problem-based learning sessions, towards the adoption of dialogic facilitation. What I mean by dialogic facilitation is a position whereby the facilitator is able to be part of a team debate without imposing their own agenda, and can promote learning through dialogue without directing the students about what should be learnt. Wilkie's research has demonstrated that facilitators do change and adapt their role over time and that their ability to become less controlling and directing is related to their pedagogical beliefs. Wilkie's research indicates that on-going support is required to help facilitators to adapt their role over time, as the students become more familiar with problem-based learning and more sophisticated as learners. The provision of on-going educational development, therefore, needs to include:

Facilitator support groups

Although an initial programme of educational development may help staff to work as a team and support each other in the development of problem-based learning materials, support groups are an important focus for specific facilitator develop-ment. Such support groups can take a number of forms and all of the following have been effective:

Externally facilitated groups
When staff are new to problem-based learning and it is adopted wholesale across a curriculum, it is advisable that some external support is provided for facilitators. In this case, an external facilitator is used to guide the group through the issues that they are facing. The role of the external facilitator is to help staff to express their concerns and listen to and learn from one another, and to guide them towards

positive resolutions of issues. The value of this is that staff are helped not to spend time in the facilitated support group arguing, complaining or disagreeing, but instead are enabled to use the time in a way that is constructive and will help them, their colleagues and the curriculum to move forward. This type of group usually takes place once a month for an hour over the first six months of the course and then is reduced over time depending on the needs of the staff involved.

Leaderless groups

Staff may decide that they would prefer to have a support group that is not facilitated, is voluntary and is managed by the facilitators themselves. What is important here is that meetings are set regularly and an agenda is organized in advance, so that the meeting does not just comprise complaints, thereby resulting in staff becoming disgruntled. It is also important that meetings are scheduled over a short time, for example meeting on alternate weeks for eight weeks, at the end of which the purpose and function of the group is reviewed. This will enable staff to keep focused on the issues and encourage staff to attend each session. Leaderless groups often fail because they are scheduled over too long a period of time and with too little focus.

Action learning sets

Here the facilitators meet in groups of six to eight to deal with the issue of becoming facilitators and the challenges that this has brought to them personally and pedagogically. These sets are ideal for both providing support and resolving issues, since individuals help each other to move forward with their concerns. Furthermore, the set is more than a support group because through it staff learn about themselves, each other and problem-based learning through a continuous process of reflecting and acting on an individual's problem. However, it is important that the sets are formalized and that they meet on a regular basis to undertake action that will deal with or resolve problems.

Master classes

After staff have undertaken educational development and then implemented problem-based learning, many of them feel that support groups are helpful for resolving issues but neither help them to develop their capabilities as facilitators nor enable them to design more complex materials for problem-based learning. What has been helpful for many staff one year after the implementation of problem-based learning is a series of master classes. These are interactive workshop sessions on topics suggested by the staff but facilitated by an external expert. Topics for this may include reviewing the assessment process, developing complex trigger materials and examining the stances of staff in the facilitation process. These master classes are designed to be informative, help staff examine the latest research on the given topic and offer staff an opportunity to engage in-depth with an issue.

Communicative evaluation

Research has demonstrated that facilitators value support from each other and that such support can be a major influence in adjusting to and developing problem-based learning (Murray and Savin-Baden 2000; Wilkie 2002). However, support can also be provided through evaluation. This may take the form of peer evaluation, whereby a 'buddy system' is introduced and facilitators are put into pairs. Each member of the pair facilitates their own problem-based learning team, but they attend as many of their colleague's sessions as possible as an observer and provide feedback to their colleague on what was helpful about the way in which they facilitated and what could be improved upon. A buddy system, together with formal and informal opportunities for staff to evaluate their own and colleagues' progress as facilitators, can promote communicative action. Niemi and Kemmis (1999) have suggested that communicative evaluation of teaching practice can provide a means of enhancing educational opportunities for all parties concerned. They stated that the process of sustaining and creating communicative action produces mutual understanding and unforced consensus around a programme, while providing the potential for future development.

Facilitator rejuvenation

The implementation of problem-based learning in many countries first began in the 1980s and many of the staff involved in that implementation are still using problem-based learning, albeit not in the same university. Over the last few years, there has been an emerging discussion about what has been termed 'facilitator burn-out' or 'facilitator fatigue'. To date there has been little, if any, research into this, but what is being described is a position whereby problem-based learning facilitators have become tired, bored and dissatisfied with facilitation. There are several ways of dealing with this. The first is that when implementing problem-based learning initially, it is important to plan an educational development programme for as many staff as possible, but not to use them all as facilitators at the outset. Ideally, facilitators should be involved with problem-based learning for three years and then spend time away from problem-based learning, teaching on other parts of the programme, doing research or taking on a more administrative role for at least a year. Few problem-based programmes use this approach exclusively and many choose to use lectures, skills sessions, fieldwork and other approaches to provide diversity for students. Facilitator burn-out occurs most among staff who value and enjoy problem-based learning and who often facilitate too many teams or feel they have to do more problem-based learning than anything else because other staff refuse to get involved. A solution may be to have a dedicated team of facilitators for a three-year period who do little other teaching on the programme and then replace them all at once with another dedicated team. Managing the facilitation within the curriculum is an important area that needs to be considered before problem-based learning is implemented.

It could be argued that what I am suggesting is costly, demanding and inappropriate in the current climate of higher education, but such strategies have and are being used in the UK. These have enabled staff not only to implement problem-based learning but have also, to date, prevented facilitator burn-out. In several problem-based programmes, where facilitators are not encouraged to develop their capabilities or to take time away from facilitation to rejuvenate and evaluate their progress, burn-out has occurred.

Ensuring quality learning

What counts as quality learning and for whom is a complex set of concerns to unpack. Due to the constant focus on accountability, quality assurance and value for money, it is important to consider the kinds of strategies facilitators have used to deal with students' concerns about the quality of their learning. Furthermore, given that problem-based learning is often criticized for offering the students too much autonomy and not ensuring that they have covered the content, it is important to examine how we know that students have learned and that they have learned quality material. There are several ways of doing this, many of which relate not just to problem-based learning but also to principles of curriculum design in general. Some of these might include:

- Using a trigger at the beginning of the course or module that encourages students to access materials from a variety of sources: magazines, pamphlets, the worldwide web, journals, textbooks and television. They are then asked to evaluate what counts as quality information and to justify their claims.
- Using debate and questioning within the problem-based learning team to promote critical questioning of each other's work and presentations. Instead of students feeding back their researched materials to the team, criticality will be promoted through the summarizing and critiquing of their findings and raising questions for debate.
- Ensuring that the cohort convene on a regular basis, so that each problem-based learning team can present their strategy or solution and they can critique each other's work.
- Using assessment approaches that will ensure students undertake quality work within the team that is then rewarded with both a team and an individual summative mark.
- Adopting summative peer assessment so that the teams and their members are accountable to one another and become critical about each other's work.
- Ensuring that assessment approaches match rather than undermine the problem-based learning, so that students can see the relationship between learning and assessment.
- Acknowledging that a team is not functioning well; it is important not to ignore this and hope the problems will resolve themselves. Ask the team to evaluate the way they are functioning as a team and, if necessary, use questionnaires or diagnostic tools to help them evaluate their roles and progress.

- Asking a colleague or fellow student from a different team to join the session to give feedback on the way the team is functioning and being facilitated.

Ensuring that students learn effectively through problem-based learning requires that the trigger materials are well designed and that the assessment methods match the form of learning. It remains surprising that the number of difficulties that emerge in problem-based curricula are because the problem situations students are expected to explore are too simplistic or directive, resulting in students not engaging with the learning but instead just trying to discover the answers that they believe the tutor wants. If students are to own their own learning and develop independence in inquiry, the problem scenarios presented to them need to encourage these practices. A useful strategy might be to ask staff to design materials using a problem scenario taxonomy, such as that delineated by Schmidt and Moust (2000). Assessment methods must then support these practices further by encouraging students to take a stance towards the knowledge they have been taught and offering critical perspectives upon it. Short answer questions, multiple-choice questions and examinations can restrict such learning opportunities and it is important that curriculum design is acknowledged as a central component of ensuring quality learning for students on problem-based programmes. It is also important that the team works effectively together and understands its role and purpose, and that the facilitator is sensitive about group process but also prepared to challenge the members when poor or inaccurate work is presented.

Equipping staff for facilitation in diverse contexts

There continues to be a debate about what counts as problem-based learning and what does not. This has brought with it a number of problems relating to educational development for problem-based learning. For example, in some universities something that I would refer to as small-group teaching is referred to as problem-based learning. Additionally, students working in groups of four in a tiered lecture theatre, discussing questions the lecturer has raised as a result of a short talk he has given, has also been termed problem-based learning, whereas I would see this as an interactive lecture. The lines between different forms of interactive learning, small-group teaching and problem-based learning will inevitably remain blurred. However, it is important to understand the purpose for which we are equipping facilitators. Although it is important for all facilitators to undergo educational development at the outset, dealing with different constructions of problem-based learning demands different capabilities. For example, if problem-based learning is being undertaken by students in a first-year module with a large cohort of students (say 150–180), and it has been decided to conduct it in a large classroom with students in groups of five around tables with a roving facilitator, then this facilitator will need to be equipped for such an approach. One facilitator managing a single group of ten students in one dedicated room is a completely different challenge. Small-group problem-based learning can result in an intense and sometimes co-dependent relationship between facilitator and group; confusion can arise between the role of the facilitator and that of the personal tutor, so that lines become blurred between students' personal and pedagogical problems. In contrast, in large-group problem-based learning, there are opportunities for students to avoid undertaking the work, individually or corporately, attendance is difficult to monitor, the room will be noisy and the facilitator will be required to facilitate many small groups at the same time, with feedback becoming complex and difficult. It is therefore important when designing any module that the educational development provided prepares staff for either a range of ways of utilizing problem-based learning or is specifically focused at the type to be used.

Diversity does not just include different formations or models of problem-based learning, but also issues connected with students' experience, ability, background, race and culture. I have heard the argument that problem-based learning does not work well with particular groups of students in specific countries. Yet when I meet lecturers from these countries who are using problem-based learning, many argue that it is the staff who have difficulty in adapting and not the students. MacKinnon has made a pertinent point:

> One of the most important lessons to be learned from the Hong Kong experience is that students seem to have less difficulty adapting to a PBL [problem-based learning] curriculum than do academic staff. We found that students' ability to transcend their cultural inhibitions and prior edu- cational experiences was related to how well the conversion was managed. The challenge, therefore, lies in properly managing the process of curriculum reform.
>
> (MacKinnon 1999)

Dealing with diversity in problem-based learning is no different from dealing with it in other areas of the curriculum: it requires sound preparation, awareness of students with difficulties, sensitivity to differences and honesty with ourselves and our students about what is possible within the organization and culture in which we are operating.

Conclusion

Supporting and developing facilitators in the context of problem-based learning continues to be a complex area and a demanding task. Institutional learning and teaching strategies, understandings of what counts as problem-based learning and perceptions about the kinds of support that should be provided for facilitators will have an impact on the way in which problem-based learning is implemented and sustained, whether terrestrially or virtually.

7

Virtual Facilitation

Introduction

Online learning and distance education have seen major development since the late 1980s. There are modules and programmes that use different forms of online learning to support problem-based learning but few, if any, to date that are wholly problem-based. In this chapter, current notions of facilitation will be examined with regard to virtual environments and new forms of learning communities. In particular, it will explore current and emerging trends in the use of computer-mediated and multimedia problem-based learning and present a possibility for using problem-based learning online that marries the principles of problem-based learning with online learning.

Online education

Online education is a growth area in education but many of the frustrations in universities stem from the expense of new equipment, the speed of change and the need for continual updating. Universities have tight budgets and securing funds for new systems to support online learning is a constant battleground. Many universities have a team of developers to design online education with technicians in support; others have a few keen academics in a cupboard. There continue to be debates, too, about the form and content of online education and this has been captured by Mason, who has argued that:

> Many computer-based teaching programs whether stand alone, or on an Intranet or the Web, fall into one of two categories: all glitz and no substance, or content that reflects a rote-learning, right/wrong approach to learning
>
> (Mason 1998: 4)

It could be argued that this is still very much the case in many curricula. However, the more recent focus on students as customers and approaches such as problem-based learning have forced a reappraisal and a redesigning of online education, so that it can facilitate the development of knowledge management, problem-solving, critique and learning how to learn. Mason (1998) has suggested three online course models that, although simple, do offer a way of understanding the differences in online communities and the ways in which problem-based learning fit with some models and not others.

Content + support model

In this model, course content is, in general, separate from tutorial support. Content is provided for the students either on the web or as a package of material, whereas tutorial support is given via email or computer conferencing and this support usually represents no more than 20 per cent of the students' study time. Thus in practice the online elements tend to be added on, and the course material is designed in ways that can be tutored by teachers other than those who have written the content. In this model, the notion of the development of an online community is severely restricted by the strong division between support and content. This means that students have no real sense of building up experience of working collaboratively online or supporting one another through online communication. Although the advantage of this model is that the high course development costs can be offset by low presentation costs, the possibility for collaborative working is limited. The result is that if this model is used for problem-based learning, the course is content-driven, students have little opportunity to define their own learning needs and much of the work is done by students working individually and interacting with the tutor. This then dissolves any notion of dialogic learning that is seen by many as vital to the problem-based approach.

Wrap around model

This model has been described by Mason as the 50/50 model, since here tailor-made materials are wrapped around existing materials and online interactions and discussion occupy half the students' time. Thus what we see in practice is students engaging with online activities and discussions supported by existing textbooks, CD-ROM resources and tutorials. Thus real-time events such as audio lectures are used and students interact through posting email questions. The tutor's role is more demanding, because unlike the content + support model, less of the course is predetermined and tutors are required to interact with the students through the online activities and discussions. There is a sense that this model offers students more of an online community, because screen-sharing software can be used for problem-solving components of the curriculum. This means that tutors can facilitate students on a one-to-one or small-group basis and the course is created through these interactions. The danger here, however, is that what at first seems to be problem-based learning is actually problem-solving learning, and this confusion can cause disjunction for students between the expectation of autonomy and the control exerted by the tutor.

Integrated model

In this model, online discussion, processing information and undertaking tasks are central to the course, with the consequence that course content, because the students largely determine it, is both fluid and dynamic. The course comprises learning resources, collaborative activities and joint assignments in ways that create a learning community by reducing the distinction between content and support, and promoting a course content defined by the student cohort. In practice, activities are carried out on the Web using resources supplied by tutors, external links and real-time events. The interactive nature of such courses means that students can integrate components of discussion conferences, along with personal reflections, into their assignments. This model appears to be the one that would fit most effectively with problem-based learning, but currently there is relatively little software to support collaborative problem-based learning. For example, in the integrated model, although students are involved in online activities and discussions, there is still little real sense of collaborative working – although *Knowledge Forum* is able to provide some of the collaborative opportunities afforded by terrestrial problem-based learning. There is a further concern in that terrestrial problem-based learning relies on free-for-all discussions, particularly in the initial session. These types of discussions have largely been abandoned in online education, with students being provided instead with specific tasks and timelines to give them structure and promote active learning. Thus unless real-time communication is initiated by students, there is relatively little opportunity for dialogic, student-centred learning to emerge.

Computer-mediated communication and problem-based learning

With the shift towards a mass higher education system in the UK, and the growing use of computer-mediated communication in higher education globally, there has been an increasing demand for the use of problem-based learning in this field. Using computer-mediated communication with distance learners was initially seen as having the ideal of 'a collaborative respectful interdependence, where the student takes responsibility for personal meaning as well as creating mutual understanding in a learning community' (Garrison 1993: 17). Given that in problem-based learning collaborative learning is seen as one of the key features of the approach, it might appear at first that computer-mediated problem-based learning is a retrograde step. There is a certain sense that working and learning face-to-face in teams is vital to the process of problem-based learning. The face-to-face negotiation, collaboration and debate characteristic of problem-based learning is seen to equip students to manage the multiple frameworks of understanding, action and self-identity that they will need in a changing and flexible labour market. Initially, I was sceptical about computer-mediated problem-based learning. My mistrust went something like: 'what is the point of using problem-based learning electronically as you can't really work in teams that way?' Yet it soon became apparent that the debate was not about problem-based learning versus computer-mediated learning, but more a question of how best it could be facilitated. The advantages that are often missed when linking these two approaches are:

- Changes in university cultures (such as split-site campuses and universities with large student numbers) mean that computer-mediated problem-based learning offers students space to learn in teams even though they may be dispersed geographically.
- Computer-mediated problem-based learning creates a new type of learning community that is different from real-time problem-based learning teams.
- It is sometimes easier to challenge and confront peers through computer-mediated problem-based learning than it is to do so face-to face. It has been argued that computer-mediated communication can provide more intense communication than face-to-face teams, where the lack of social pressure and the greater freedom to express views without struggling for the right of audience enables participants to react to the content, and not the author, with more reflective and effective communications (Henri and Rigault 1996: 10).
- Computer-mediated problem-based learning often provides more opportunity for 'reflective and thoughtful analysis and review of earlier contributions' (Kaye 1992: 17).

Thus computer-mediated problem-based learning can help students to use team conferences as an additional central communication space, as a place for sharing and examining individual perspectives and as a place to manage the work and administration of the team interaction. Computer-mediated problem-based learning is an area of growth and development and one we should not ignore, since by combining both forms of learning multiple advantages occur for both staff and students. However, it is also important to delineate the different ways in which computer-mediated learning is being used with problem-based learning. While acknowledging that language and technology is changing daily in this sphere, it is important to have some clarity about the ways in which it is currently being used and what this might mean for students and facilitators.

Forms of virtual problem-based learning

The term 'computer-mediated problem-based learning' has been used initially to define any form of problem-based learning that utilizes computers in some way. However, this is problematic, since it offers little indication about the ways in which computers are being used, the areas of interaction of the students, the quality of the learning materials or the extent to which any of these fit with problem-based learning. Furthermore, other issues need to be taken into account, such as developing tutors' online facilitation capabilities, providing some synchronous events to support students, encouraging collaborative interactive participation and finding ways of engaging students who seldom participate in the online problem-based learning team.

To understand these complexities, it is important to examine what is on offer and to explore the fit between the approach and type of problem-based learning that is adopted. For example, it is difficult to marry some forms of computer-mediated problem-based learning with types of problem-based learning that seek to provide opportunities for the students to challenge, evaluate and interrogate models of action, knowledge, reasoning and reflection, such as problem-based learning for critical contestability (Savin-Baden 2000a).

Computer simulation in problem-based learning

Rendas *et al.* (1999) introduced a computer simulation that was designed for problem-based learning to motivate learning, structure knowledge in a clinical context and develop learning skills for medical students at a stage in the programme when they had had little contact with patients. It was also designed to evaluate how students reasoned and learned in each session. The problem situation provided all the information about a patient in a predetermined sequence and students, working three to a computer, were expected to find out further information by asking one question at a time, seeking justification for the hypothesis they had put forward and being encouraged to identify learning issues. The answers provided by the students were logged and later analysed with a tutor. The difficulty with this particular model of computer simulation is that it offers students little opportunity for creativity and personal responsibility and in many ways resembles some of the earlier forms of guided discovery. For example, guided discovery methods used with linear problem-solving models guided students to the right answers. In several medical and health-related curricula that use computer simulations in the context of problem-based learning this process can be seen. What is really occurring here is that problem-solving learning is being used to guide students to the right answer or diagnosis. An example of this would be the virtual autopsy developed by Leicester Warwick Medical School. This is an innovative and effective tool that has proved to be a useful way of learning for students. However, it is essentially diagnostic in nature and thus students follow a step-by-step approach to solve a problem that encourages reductionist rather than constructivist forms of learning. This is fine if it is presented as problem-solving learning and it is acknowledged that problem situations have just been designed around disciplines or diseases. Yet in many cases it is referred to as computer-aided or computer-simulated problem-based learning, which causes confusions for staff, students and those seeking to imitate this approach in other disciplines or institutions.

A different model used at the University of Central England Learning Methods Unit is a simulation developed for academic staff to learn about university policies and procedures in an innovative and interesting way. Staff are given a problem situation in a fictitious university with a somewhat stereotyped bunch of academic staff who are trying to improve student numbers in the business school. The difficulty with this type of simulation is that it can be seen as a game-playing environment in which there appears to be few objectives or outcomes. Furthermore, the way that the scenario has been designed to gain staff interest has brought with it three other difficulties. The first is that the scenario is so large and complex, with a vast array of learning objectives, that it feels overwhelming to tackle. The second difficulty is that the use of stereotypes is distracting when this does not really appear to be part of the pedagogy of the problem situation. The final difficulty is that the simulation has been designed for staff to focus on individual rather than col-laborative ways of problem management.

A more recent development has been the use of neighbourhood simulation at the University of Teesside School of Health and Social Care. Here nursing students act as community nurses who deal with scenarios that happen to members of the virtual neighbourhood. As illness, accidents, bereavements and life events occur within the neighbourhood, students are asked to explore their role as nurses and the kinds of intervention they may offer. They are also asked to examine the impact one family may have on another in the context of a community. The advantage with this model is that it can be adapted from year to year, is based on real-life situations and can be responsive to local and national issues.

An important advantage of problem-based learning is the way in which it pro-motes dialogic learning and thus such an advantage is lost when staff or students work alone at a computer and do not discuss the scenario with peers. It may seem that the use of computer simulation is ill-advised, but in fact this is not the case. All problem scenarios in problem-based learning curricula need to be well designed and tested before use and it is the same with computer simulations. However, I would argue that a computer simulation is better used as a component of a scenario, rather than the scenario itself, so that some of the difficulties of games and simulations noted here can be avoided. Simulations need to be located within problem-based learning rather than used as a mechanism or strategy to try to promote problem-based learning.

Multimedia resources for problem-based learning

Multimedia resources in problem-based learning tend to mirror the content + support model of online education, since they are used to support existing course material. In some virtual learning environments, they are accessed as an integral part of a learning package but to date the inclusion of videos, small-scale simula-tions and lectures are primarily the extent of what has been utilized. Although the technology does exist to produce the kind of multimedia learning that offers students choices, challenges and interesting ways to learn, the range of audio, video and text materials is often very expensive to prepare.

Virtual learning environments in problem-based learning

Virtual learning environments are learning management software systems that are not intended to merely replace the classroom online, but instead to offer learners a variety of options to facilitate learning. Many advocates of these environments see in them the potential for allowing student-centred learning to be incorporated into their teaching in new and innovative ways. The use of terminology relating to these environments tends to be predominantly pedagogically driven, but the term 'virtual learning environment' is used here to include learning management systems and online learning environments. Thus virtual learning environments are learning management software systems that synthesize computer-mediated communications software, such as email and online course materials.

While the number of systems available is large, many of them have similar features and, although they are, in general, designed to promote varied and effective teaching styles, there are a number of limitations that apply to collaborative forms of learning. Most systems are capable of supporting content-driven online education, but there is little data to indicate which systems can support problem-based learning effectively. However, some authors (Crawley 1999; Britain and Liber 2000) have advocated the use of Laurillard's conversational model (Laurillard 1993) as a means of evaluating virtual learning environments, since it can be used to examine constructivist and conversational approaches to learning. This model contains key characteristics that mirror some of the processes involved in problem-based learning:

- *Discursive*: teachers' and learners' conceptions are accessible to each other, they agree learning goals for the topic and students receive feedback on discussion related to the topic goal.
- *Adaptive*: the teacher uses the relationship between their own and the students' conceptions to guide the dialogue.
- *Interactive*: the students take responsibility for achieving the goal and the teacher provides feedback on the actions.
- *Reflective*: the teacher supports the process whereby students link the feedback on their actions to the topic goal for each level of description within the structure of the topic

Although this model has considerable use as a device for evaluating computer-mediated problem-based learning, it is problematic for two reasons. First, the focus is largely on teacher guidance and direction, rather than developing student autonomy and peer discussion. Second, it only really deals with interactions between a single student and a teacher, and thus omits peer group interaction and the tools required by the teacher to facilitate a number of students.

However, having just discussed several of these innovations and their link with problem-based learning, I would argue that we need a term that captures the essence and advantages of both virtual learning environments and problem-based learning contexts. Thus I will argue here that we need to develop 'computer-mediated *collaborative* problem-based learning' (CMCPBL).

Computer-mediated collaborative problem-based learning

This conception of problem-based learning places it pedagogically in a collaborative online environment and thus it has a number of advantages over models mentioned earlier. While many of the current models of online education focus on teacher-centred learning, CMCPBL needs to be focused on a team-orientated knowledge-building discourse. Scardemalia and Bereiter (1994) have defined three characteristics of this discourse:

1. A focus of problem scenarios and depth of understanding.
2. Open knowledge-building that focuses on collective knowledge so that inquiry is driven by a quest for understanding.
3. An inclusion of all participants in the broader knowledge community, thus learning involves students, teachers, administrators, researchers, curriculum designers and assessors. This brings a wide range of perspectives and an acknowledgement that anything done by one person means that others must adapt.

The impact of the inclusion of these three characteristics means that learners and facilitators may take on different roles in the course of a collaborative learning situation, which again brings online education of this sort in line with the dialogic nature of problem-based learning. Before ways are suggested as to how this might be achieved in practice, it is first important to define CMCPBL and offer suggestions of how it might be implemented.

Computer-mediated collaborative problem-based learning is defined here as students working in teams of eight to ten on a series of problem scenarios that combine to make up a module. Students are expected to work collaboratively to solve or manage the problem. Students will work in real-time or asynchronously, but what is important is that they work together. Synchronous collaboration tools are vital for the effective use of CMCPBL because tools such as chat, shared whiteboards, video conferencing and group browsing are central to ensuring collaboration within the problem-based learning team.

Students may be working at a distance or on campus, but they will begin by working out what they need to learn to engage with the problem situation. This may take place through a shared whiteboard, conferencing or an email discussion group. What is also important is that students have both access to the objectives of the module and also the ability to negotiate their own learning needs in the context of the given outcomes. Facilitation occurs through the tutor having access to the on-going discussions without necessarily participating in them. Tutors also plan real-time sessions with the CMCPBL team to engage with the discussion and facilitate the learning.

A model of a CMCPBL session for a team of eight students engaging in a scenario that takes place over a three-week period and is supported by some video lectures may be presented in the following way:

- Scenarios are designed by staff for the module and are constantly online so that the students can see what is planned for the module as a whole.
- Students open the tutorial conference where the scenario and any resources are situated. These resources should be limited so that students are not directed towards particular material and instead develop their own list of learning needs.
- Students should be encouraged to read the scenario before coming online, so that as individuals they have considered their own learning needs.

Seminar one: introductory session

At a prescribed time in the first week, the members of a team meet with the facilitator for a 'private chat', in short, a facilitated online problem-based learning seminar. The scenario may be discussed for about 60–90 minutes, during which the tutor helps students to define their learning needs while also checking understanding and ensuring that students have shared out the tasks fairly around the team. However, the skill required of the tutor in this session is in not intervening too soon, thereby enabling students to make their own decisions about their learning needs.

In cases where students are new to problem-based learning or even CMCPBL, it is advisable that they are encouraged to use a shared whiteboard during meetings, so that they can reflect on their progress in preparation for the next tutorial.

In advance of the second seminar, a week after the first one, students are expected to upload their own material to share with the rest of the team. This needs to be done before the second seminar so that students have time to read the materials and tutors can examine what has been uploaded.

Seminar two: feedback session

At a prescribed time, the members of the team meet the tutor again and, having read the materials that have been uploaded, they debate and ask questions of each other and seek clarification on materials not understood. The latter part of the seminar is spent working out how to apply this material to the original problem scenario, and to check whether there have been any omissions in the researched materials that need to be addressed. Between the second and third seminar, students will be expected to work asynchronously or in scheduled discussion decided by them to apply the researched material. Students present back to the tutor what they believe is a solution or a means of managing the problem situation in advance of the third seminar.

Seminar three: discussion and co-construction

This final seminar is a discussion between tutors and students of what has been presented, with the tutor offering feedback and the students reflecting on the process. This seminar can be synchronous or asynchronous.

An example of such a form of CMCPBL can be seen at Glasgow Caledonian University. This is a one-year conversion course for qualified nurses who require the further qualification of mental health nurse, and is undertaken at a distance. A further example is at Dublin Institute of Technology, where a CMCPBL module in Teaching in Higher Education has been implemented for lecturers undertaking the certificate in learning and teaching (Donnelly 2002). However, there are issues that need to be considered when designing these new environments.

Virtual pedagogies and (re)distributed facilitation?

For students, the shift to new forms of learning, different from more traditional didactic approaches they have experienced in school and further education, is often challenging. The introduction of problem-based learning and computer-mediated learning introduces students to two new elements of learning. This has an impact not only on the problem-based learning and computer-mediated learning, but also on other forms of learning within the curriculum. There are few curricula where problem-based learning is used as the only approach to learning and increasingly students have to manage not only the interplay of knowledge across modules but also different approaches to learning. However, there are also issues about the reasons for using CMCPBL in the first place. For example, it is questionable as to whether there is value in using real-time CMCPBL for students undertaking the same programme at the same university, unless it is used because of long distances between campus sites where students are using the same problem-based learning scenario. Questions also need to be asked about whether having asynchronous teams adds something different to CMCPBL. Certainly in distance education, across time zones and campus sites, this would be useful and suit different students' lives and working practices. Yet this raises problems about how cooperative and collaborative it is possible to be, in terms of sharing learning and ideas and developing forms of learning that are genuinely dialogic in nature.

A further issue relates less to how CMCPBL is enacted in practice and more to the preparation of materials. Considerable time and effort goes into the preparation and design of online materials, but in the context of problem-based learning there needs to be a real clarity about how scenarios are created so that they produce robust educational discussion. Wegner *et al.* (1999) used a problem-based model to compare two groups of students undertaking a two-year advanced level curriculum design and evaluation programme. Both the experimental group and control group used problem-based learning. The control group used communication technology that included telephone, fax, email and research websites. Students in the experimental group utilized an instructional management system, TopClass. The findings indicated that the use of an instruction management system for the delivery of distance learning had a positive effect on internet-based communication by students. This suggests that such systems, linked with problem-based learning, could promote inter-student communication more effectively than CMCPBL, which does not use instructional management systems. However, Wegner *et al.* did not evaluate the problem-based learning component of this programme.

It would appear that different types of scenarios may need to be used in online education than those used in terrestrial problem-based learning, ones that are pedagogically different, because online communication is more complex than face-to-face communication in small teams. Furthermore, it might also be that online education results in a particular typology of problem-based learning that requires different scenarios. At one level, the inter-linking of problem-based learning with virtual learning environments has brought creativity to problem-based learning and the development of innovative multimedia materials. However, it is clear from much of the literature that this is not always the case, and the focus on the achievement of outcomes and tasks is causing instead a narrowing of the definition of problem-based learning and a certain boundedness about the types of problem scenarios being adopted and the way that problem-based learning is being used.

In earlier chapters, the notion of facilitation at different levels has been discussed and in particular what might count as effective facilitation. Salmon has provided a comprehensive guide to 'e-moderating': an electronic moderator is someone who 'presides over an electronic online meeting or conference' (Salmon 2000: 3). She draws on research on staff and students' perspectives, offers guidance on training e-moderators and suggests a useful model for teaching through computer-mediated collaboration. However, there has been little documented in the literature about the role of the facilitator in computer-mediated problem-based learning. For some, there is an assumption that when eight students share a computer to engage with a scenario, that it is sufficient for a roving tutor to call round briefly to each team. Yet this does not mirror the current notions of problem-based learning facilitation and, in many ways, downgrades the role of the facilitator in a problem-based learning team. A virtual model of facilitation that reflects some of the best terrestrial problem-based learning facilitation practices is required. Here, for example, a facilitator could join in the email debates students are having and call in on discussions. Yet there are problems, too, with this in terms of staff time and students' participation. For example, how do we deal with students who do not participate in CMCPBL? There is a tendency to use quantitative forms of computer-assisted assessment with problem-based learning such as QuestionMark, which does not mirror the process of problem-based learning and could cause difficulties over participation and collaboration in many problem-based teams.

Conclusion

The diversity and complexity of online and distance education means that it is problematic to utilize computer-mediated collaborative problem-based learning pedagogically in the curriculum and in higher education in general. What it means to facilitate in a virtual context will depend upon a number of factors that include the type of online learning, the values about the type of facilitation that is required and the extent to which students are encouraged to develop student–student inter-action through such programmes. As we have seen, there are several difficulties in attempting to implement CMCPBL. In the main, these appear to be related to the kind of virtual learning environments available, the way in which small group learning can be utilized in a distributed form, ways of promoting and rewarding student–student interaction rather than student–tutor interaction, and the challenges around developing scenarios that support the pedagogical aims of problem-based learning and meet the needs of online learning. The difficulties documented here are reflected not only in the literature but also in the lack of modules globally that use CMCPBL. Although other forms of problem-based learning are being used online, it is the collaboration and dialogue that needs to be developed further by and within the online community.

8

Beyond Surveillance: Assessment and Facilitation

A few months ago, I was reading the dialogue that was taking place on a problem-based learning discussion list. The arguments centred on whether or not examinations were an appropriate method of assessing problem-based learning, and whether in fact multiple-choice questions were better than the more traditional short answer questions. I sat at my desk, yet again feeling puzzled. I wondered, not for the first time, how such methods of assessment could be matched with a method of learning that I believed required not only a different way of thinking about teaching and learning, but also of thinking about assessment. As I reflected on the discussions I have had on this issue over the years with many tutors, I realized that there were a range of inconsistencies about how assessment is seen and undertaken in many curricula, not just those that are problem-based.

Introduction

This chapter unpacks the relationship between assessment and facilitation. I argue here that although assessment has been discussed widely in relation to problem-based learning, few of the difficulties have been solved and that relatively little has been discussed about the role of the facilitator in relation to group, peer and self-assessment. I also examine the interrelationship of tutors' self-assessment, students' rating of tutors and students' perceptions of the facilitators.

Dilemmas in assessment

Issues about the impact of assessment on student learning, both on traditional and problem-based curricula, has been the subject of much debate and education research (Boud 1990; Gibbs 1992). Many of the concerns about assessment in higher education appear to relate to the unintended side-effects that undermine or contradict staff intentions to encourage students to learn effectively. Such side-effects include rote memorization at the expense of understanding, description rather than critique, attendance only at sessions that are being assessed or provide cues to assessment criteria, issues of fairness and the clarity of marking criteria. Yet the issue of assessment seems to be bound up not just with the idea of assessing what it is that staff want students to learn in higher education, but with many of the values implicit with being a student in higher education. We seem to get confused between assessing knowledge and skill and imbuing a sense of the progression of learning about the discipline in students. It is the conflicts that arise between these coded practices that confuse our students. What I mean is that we often focus on covering content and checking that students have key skills, so that these are the things that students perceive to have most value. For many of us, assessment is part of the learning and is designed to help students progress to another (higher) level of learning, yet we rarely make this explicit or find ways of enabling students to see assessment as part of their learning journey. For them, assessment is often about being strategic, cue-conscious and decoding what is really required. Harris (2001) has suggested that plagiarism often occurs because students do not understand what is required of them in assessment, and has argued that tutors need to make both the intentions and the language used in assessment clear to students.

Across the literature on both assessment and problem-based learning, we see arguments about the relative values of the *types* of assessment we are using. The result is that we confuse typology with purpose. For example, there is a kind of implicit view that essays are somehow better than examinations or that peer assessment is better than short answer questions. While there are arguments and research to suggest that this may be the case, there is a sense that to argue this is missing the point. What we are doing is confusing form with purpose, so that when designing a curriculum we tend to explore the type of assessments that will match the learning approach. This is good and sound practice, but we do not often examine the underlying purpose of the assessment. For example, the assessment may be to test knowledge, equip the student with particular skills or quite starkly it may be to ensure that they have enough grasp of the subject to pass from one year to the next. While many of us espouse the matching of learning with assessment, there is not always a realization – or, perhaps, at worst an honesty – about the underlying purpose of an assessment.

Thus we can see that assessment is fraught with difficulties. At one level there is the assumption that if there is a fit between learning methods, the course objectives and the assessment, then there will be few problems. At another, authors such as Heron (1988) and Usher and Edwards (1994) would have us believe that we cannot assess anyone without falling into hegemonic practices. This may be rather an oversimplification of the issues but there are concerns here.

With the first assumption, we are faced with the continually recurring theme in many of the articles and chapters on assessment, that there is a tendency to ignore the subject in which the student is being assessed. In recent years, there has been discussion about situated learning, learning in context and, more recently, critique of learning inventories that decontextualize learner and learning (Haggis 2002), and yet there seem to be few debates about the notion of context in the assessment process. I do not mean whether the assessment is taking place in an examination hall or on a glacier. I mean that we forget about the subject area in which the assessment is situated, and the impact that this has on how the assessment has been devised, what is expected of the assessment and of the students, and how knowledge is seen within that subject, as well as the type and purpose of assessment. So often assessment is talked about as if it is something we can decontextualize from universities, curriculum design, subject area, staff and students. It is only in examining our assumptions, theories and practices that we can begin to understand how to gain some kind of constructive alignment (Biggs 1999) between learning and assessment. Biggs has suggested that teaching needs to be a balanced system in which all components support one another:

> If we specify our objectives in terms of understanding, we need a theory of understanding in order to define what we mean; in deciding on teaching methods that address the objectives we need a theory of learning and teaching. Hence, constructive alignment is a marriage between a constructivist understanding of the nature of learning, and an aligned design for teaching.
>
> (Biggs 1999: 26)

What is problematic about Biggs' argument here is the notion of defining what we mean, and how we gather all the constructivists involved in the curriculum together to design something which results in a workable marriage, rather than a deconstructed one. Constructivism centres on the belief that realities are understood in the form of multiple constructions that are socially and experientially based. Thus if we are to adopt Biggs' notion wholeheartedly, then curricula can only really be designed through the interaction between tutor and students. We do not have a curriculum. It is constructed with and through our students. Therefore, we also do not have assessments but have to formulate them interactionally. If then within our curriculum the aims and goals are spoken of in terms of an abiding concern for the life world, then we need to examine the process of meaning construction with our subjects and disciplines, and clarify how meanings are embodied within these and in the language used by staff and students. Thus the types of questions we would ask include: 'What does knowing mean in this context?' 'How do we create a curriculum that engages in the construction and development of that knowing?'

Curricula where problem-based learning is central to the learning are in fact largely constructivist in nature because students do, to a large extent, make decisions about what counts as knowledge and knowing. However, what continually undermines such learning is the assessment processes, which at worst are surveillance games and at best would appear to meet some of the ideals of constructive alignment that Biggs espouses (without necessarily being constructivist *per se*).

This brings us to the second assumption, which is that of the underlying purposes and constructions associated with our assessments. Heron (1988) has argued that the prevailing model for assessing students in higher education is thought to be an authoritarian one. Thus it is all a question of power, since traditional academic arguments suggest that students are not competent to participate in determining either their 'academic destiny' or their own competence. Such unilateral control by staff is at odds with the process of education and ultimately breeds intellectual and vocational conformity in students. Heron has suggested that what is required is a redistribution of educational power, so that components of the curriculum become matters of staff–student consultation. However, Heron suggests that some parts would be non-negotiable, as they represent educational principles which staff believe are important and thus they are ones to which, as part of the course, students are invited to subscribe. Heron's arguments are persuasive and interesting, but in the current climate of performative values will be difficult to implement in some subjects. However, Usher and Edwards (1994) offer a further perspective on the issue of power in assessment of students' work. They have argued, drawing on the work of Foucault (1979), that institutions of education are important sites of regulation in modern social formations. Lecturers, therefore, are not only agents of, but also subject to, the disciplinary process of the assessment and measurement of individuals. The notion of objective measurement is thus seen as a natural process, a normalizing process which students (as subjects) have to accept and thus they become classified objects who have been measured and also subjectified, because of becoming subjects who learn the truth about themselves (Usher and Edwards 1994).

Usher and Edwards have also argued that some forms of continuous assessment, rather than being more student-centred than other traditional approaches to assessment, can be interpreted as a mechanism through which the process of surveillance is refined. What we see, in this situation, is that the students focus purely on the learning goals that are deeply embedded in the assessment criteria. Surveillance comes not necessarily through direct encounters with tutors, but instead through the performance criteria that appear to be empowering because they are available, and because students can see what they are expected to know. For example, it is expected that because students have the competences in their hands, they will understand what to do and how to do it and will thus be empowered. However, this too is problematic, since although they may look access-ible, behavioural and achievable, 'Competences are cast in behavioural terms but the discourse is itself not behaviourist. It is precisely because it is not, but rather interwoven with liberal humanist discourse that it is powerful' (Usher and Edwards 1994: 110).

What occurs in fact are hegemonic practices, practices whereby ideas, structures and actions are constructed and promoted by the powerful to maintain the *status quo*, and these come to be seen by most people as working for their own good. Examining such practices can offer us a way of understanding some of the coded practices that underpin our assessment processes. If we get as far as being clear about the underlying purpose of assessment, we then have to examine the assump-tions that go with particular disciplines. Those employed within a university are usually lecturers who teach within their discipline and utilize external examiners from that discipline. Thus the codes, practices and understandings of the discipline are maintained through teaching, assessment and quality mechanisms. Yet there is much to learn across different disciplines about the ways in which these disciplines use the same assessment. Take, for example, the essay. In English, students learn to write like English academics through the form of an essay. They learn about style, structure, linguistic devices and ways of presenting their argument; it is a medium through which they present their point of view at the same time as learning about the values of the discipline. In nursing, an essay comes with a different set of practices. Here, for example, students would be expected to demonstrate their understanding of a body of knowledge and the practical application of that knowledge to their own practice as nurses. It is seen, often, as a means of helping student nurses both to link theory and practice and also to examine them in a way that will better equip them for the world of work.

Thus we can see that many of the difficulties in assessment in problem-based learning stem not only from this approach to learning, but also because we are trying to apply generalizable concepts and practices of assessment that fit with problem-based learning across diverse disciplines with different values and practices. To begin to understand assessment issues in depth, we need to understand some of the codes, values and practices that occur in higher education, so that we can begin to see ways of getting a fit between problem-based learning, the purpose of assessment and the practice of assessment in the subject area in which it is being employed. However, before we explore these concerns, it is important to consider some of the underlying suppositions that relate to the broader role of assessment in higher education.

Paradigmatic assumptions

Our assumptions give meaning and purpose to what we do and as such they affect the way in which we teach our students and assess the work they produce. This may sound obvious, but how often do we really examine the assumptions that we bring to bear when assessing a piece of work? Brookfield (1995) has suggested that our paradigmatic assumptions are the structuring axioms that we use to order our world into categories. Although we may not recognize them as assumptions, arguing instead that they are facts we know to be true, they are in fact our paradigmatic assumptions. To question our paradigmatic assumptions is challenging and often occurs as result of some form of disjunction, but if they are examined and changed, then the impact on our teaching and perspectives can be considerable. For example, if we have always believed that sound adult educational practices are essentially democratic and that problem-based learning promotes such ideals, to discover that this is merely based on an assumption we have held for years, together with idealistic postgraduate teaching that we have received, then this can be a shock. To discover instead a world beyond adult education, such as medical education, where 'learning by humiliation' (Majoor 1999) is still relatively common, forces a reappraisal not only of a view of the education of doctors, but also of how those who teach medical students conceptualize learning.

Thus the kinds of issues that emerge, because of many of our assumptions about assessment, are such practices as the espousing of criterion-referenced assessment, and we often have the detailed criteria to show this. Yet when we are marking students' work we still subconsciously use norm-referenced approaches. While we can argue against this and believe that we do not do this, the reality can be seen explicitly in the work of external examiners who acknowledge criterion-referenced marking, but still want to see a 'spread of marks across the year group'. Our assumptions also become evident when we examine the types of answers that are deemed to be acceptable and those that are not. Many of us feel uneasy about providing students with an assessment that encourages diverse answers and is difficult to mark. Even if we do take such a risk, it is often difficult to uphold the marks we have given before our peers and, subsequently, to persuade our external examiners that such diversity is both fair and credible.

Coded practices

Hidden within our assessment procedures are many coded practices. What I mean is that because we rarely really unpack the assumptions about what it is that is being assessed, and what our assumptions are about a given assessment, we impose coded practices upon the assessment process. For example, the words used, the expectation (or lack of) at each level, the number of assessments, the opportunity for students to receive formative feedback, all these kinds of codes illustrate that in assessment the medium is also the message to the students, because it demonstrates to them what actually counts as knowledge and knowing in a given field. At the same time, the codes tell us the extent to which the knowledge offered is as given, or whether the student is allowed or encouraged to take up a position towards what has been offered. Barnett has asked:

> To what degree is the student encouraged to view the field as a dynamic process of human negotiation, storytelling, power struggle and fierce dispute? ... Is knowing – of any kind, even philosophy – understood as a form of knowing how, of knowing how to engage in and to conduct meaningful, albeit limited, transaction with others, or is it presented simply as a series of propositions and theoretical entities?
>
> (Barnett 1994: 46)

This notion of wrestling and debating with the discipline is something that appears to be lost in many of the assessments we set our students. Thus for students involved in curricula which utilize problem-based learning and who are encouraged to debate and critique knowledge and knowing in problem-based learning seminars, assessment methods that close down the opportunity to take a stance on knowledge tend to result in demotivation and frustration for students.

Many of the difficulties that arise relating to assessment stem largely from our own need to have some kind of hard evidence that the students 'know' the knowledge we have taught them or have encouraged them to learn. In many areas of higher education, particularly professional education, there is a need to ensure that students are competent to practise and there is still a tendency to over-assess. It is puzzling that if we are wanting to promote independence in inquiry and autonomy in learning that we so deeply mistrust students. At the same time as mistrusting them, there is also an assumption that if we assess them many times and in a diversity of ways, we will ensure that they are capable of attaining a degree and are competent to practise. Such assumptions illustrate misconceptions, not only about the role and purposes of assessment in learning in higher education, but also the position of assessment in forecasting competence to practise. What all this means in the context of assessment is that because we do not trust our students to be adult learners who are committed and motivated, we tend to assess problem-based learning teams. The reasoning here is to ensure attendance and commitment to the team. Some may see this as laudable, but it sits poorly with the philosophy of problem-based learning that promotes personal responsibility and autonomy.

Boundary opportunities

Although as tutors we may feel that we have little control over the assessment policies under which we are required to operate, there is a sense that by engaging with the challenges of such policies it can enable us to be creative at their boundaries. There is a confusing array of perspectives in different professions and disciplines about the possibilities for assessment in problem-based learning. Here, as in facilitation, it would appear that the boundaries of the discipline often affect what we feel is both allowable and possible with assessment practices. For example, there are those, often in the field of medical and dental education, who argue that assessment is about measuring competence and improvement through tests that are seen to be reliable. There are others who see assessment as a means of demonstrating effective learning in the curriculum, and then those who see it as a means of ensuring that students have learned. For those who see that assessment is about measuring competence and improvement, the focus on assessment will largely be about ensuring that the assessments used are good tests that give reliable results and give high face validity and, sometimes, criterion validity. One of the mechanisms that is used to ensure that they are good tests is by blueprinting them, whereby tests are checked and examined through a meticulous process to ensure content validity. Many of those who are concerned that the curriculum is effective will focus on other areas, but they will also be interested in the consequential validity of the test. Consequential validity relates to the extent to which an assessment steers learning, an issue that has become of increasing interest to those in areas such as dental and medical education, as they increasingly accept that clinical examination tends to have high face validity but low reliability. There are some (e.g. Norman 1997) who have, and continue to suggest, that it is possible to have reliable assessments, and would specifically argue for the use of multiple-choice questions as a valid and reliable way of assessing higher-order skills in problem-based programmes. However, Boud (2000) has argued that what is required is sustainable assessment, assessment that meets the needs of the present without compromising the ability of students to meet their own future learning needs.

Boud believes that the two main purposes of assessment are certification, for which summative assessment is used, and to aid learning, for which formative assessment is used. Yet he also argues that assessment needs to support learning in both summative and formative ways. However I would argue that summative assessment should aid learning more than it does currently in many problem-based programmes. This is an unnecessary distinction and the boundary between grading and learning needs to be a place for the creative development of innovative assessments for problem-based learning. The focus of assessment in problem-based learning should be on both learning and performance. In many programmes, there seems to be a separation of assessment and performance and with it the view that it is only through formative assessment that students will be helped to learn. Yet most students value the summative assessment and thus such assessment should be designed to maximize student learning and to help students to understand their value, not only in terms of grades but also in terms of seeing the development of their own learning through this process. Although it has been shown that recall of knowledge is strongly related to the match or mismatch between the context of learning and context of recall (Regehr and Norman 1996), there are still few programmes that allow students the opportunity to practise and hone their skills in multiple contexts before they are assessed; this is a lamentable omission. Instead, the trend in problem-based learning seems to be moving in several directions. The first has been that of developing assessments that particularly suit problem-based learning; the second has been the coupling of the principles of the authentic assessment movement with problem-based learning; and the third has been a drive towards the use of self, peer and collaborative assessment.

Assessments aligned to problem-based learning

To date, research has been undertaken on assessment in the field of problem-based learning to ensure that the assessment of students' performance is consistent with the teaching method, and to establish the effectiveness of problem-based learning, in particular to establish that students are acquiring abilities in problem-solving and professional competence. Activities such as the 'triple jump' (Painvin *et al.* 1979; Powles *et al.* 1981) have been developed specifically for problem-based learning, but the 'triple jump' is time-consuming and costly and tends only to be used in well-funded programmes with small student numbers. Here individual students are presented with a problem and expected to discuss the problem and their learning needs with an oral examiner. Students then locate relevant material and later discuss their findings with the examiner and are rated on problem-solving skills, self-directed learning skills and on their knowledge of the problem area. However, the 'tripartite assessment' is an approach that I have developed that appears to work effectively in a number of disciplines. It has three components:

- The team submits a report for which they receive a mark.
- The individual submits the piece of work they have researched.
- The individual writes an account of the team process that is linked to the theory of teamwork.

Together, these three components form the overall individual mark. The advantage of this is that it does not privilege team members who do less work than the others by enabling them to gain more marks as a result of being part of a team. Most students see this kind of grading as being fair. Other approaches to assessment such as essays, case-based examinations, portfolios, reports and reflective journals are commonly used and examples of the interrelationship between such methods and approaches have been discussed elsewhere (Major 2000; Macdonald and Savin-Baden 2003). However, one approach to assessment that seems to overcome some of the difficulties associated with portfolios, such as them being unwieldy and lacking in overall synthesis, is the 'patchwork text' (Winter *et al.* 1999). This is a way of getting students to present their work in written form. Students build up text in course work over several weeks. Each component of work is shared with other students and they are expected to use different styles, such as a commentary on a lecture, a personal account and a book review. This kind of assessment fits well with problem-based learning because of its emphasis on critique and self-questioning.

Authentic assessment and problem-based learning

The authentic assessment movement is being increasingly linked with problem-based learning, particularly in the USA, and is worthy of mention here, despite some of the difficulties associated with it. Authentic assessment refers to assessment that resembles reading and writing in the real world, and the aim of it is to assess students in contexts that resemble actual situations in which those abilities are required. The authentic assessment movement emerged in the 1980s and has been important in highlighting the importance of the assessment as a process rather than just as a means of grading students. The crucial underlying premise of authentic assessment is that it is said to value the thinking behind work, the process, as much as the finished product. Thus authentic assessments are expected to incorporate a wide variety of techniques 'designed to correspond as closely as possible to "real world" student experiences' (Custer 1994: 66) and are seen to have meaning in themselves when the learning they measure has value beyond the classroom and is meaningful to the learner. Thus students may be asked to evaluate case studies, write definitions and defend them orally, perform role-plays, or have oral readings recorded on tape. Much of what has been argued for in linking problem-based learning with the authentic assessment movement is little more than those arguments and ideas presented by Boud (1985, 1986). There also seems to be an authentic problem-based learning movement emerging, which appears to be arguing that problem-based learning is only really authentic if it follows the original model espoused by Barrows (see, for example, Wee and Kek 2002). The real difficulty with the arguments offered by those in the authentic assessment movement is that they want assessment to be authentic, but they are concerned that the assessment might be subjective and, therefore, they adopt tutor-centred rating scales. This concern is at odds with a form of assessment that is designed to be (subjectively) meaningful to the learner. However, the authentic movement has highlighted the importance of emphasizing both the process and product when assessing students, and in particular has encouraged staff to develop forms of assessment that are clear, concise and communicated well to students.

Self, peer and collaborative assessment

Our higher education systems do not support self and peer assessment because they largely reward students with individual grades. Many universities do not allow peer assessment to count for more than 20 per cent of the overall mark in any given module. The result is that although many students educated to work in professions are required to work and learn in teams, they are not encouraged to see the value in these forms of assessment. A further difficulty is that many staff are confused about the difference between collaborative, peer and self-assessment and use the terms together or interchangeably. Collaborative assessment is often the most appropriate starting point for both staff and students who wish to utilize methods of assessment that help students to make judgements about their own work. In collaborative assessment, the student assesses himself or herself in light of criteria agreed with the tutor. The tutor assesses the student using the same criteria and they negotiate a final grade. Self-assessment and peer assessment generally seem more daunting, because students are encouraged to develop their own criteria and have greater control over both the criteria and the grade than in collaborative assessment. Self-assessment involves identifying standards and/or criteria to apply to their work and making judgements about the extent to which they have met these criteria and standards (Boud 1986: 12). It may include essays, presentations, reports and reflective diaries. One of the difficulties with self-assessment is the tendency to make judgements about what the students meant rather than what they actually achieved. In contrast, peer assessment involves students making judgements about each other's work. This is generally used for presentations and practicals, but it can also be used for essays and exam scripts. Using peer assessment with essays is really useful with problem-based learning and also highly informative for the student and tutor. Ideally, the students design their own assessment criteria and use them to assess each other, but in many programmes they are designed by staff.

Issues for students

The impact of university requirements, that curricula are written in behavioural terms, has resulted in a struggle against competing values for those designing and implementing problem-based curricula. More recently, benchmarking and Quality Assurance Agency (QAA) requirements have resulted in a focus on content coverage and outcomes, rather than a balance of content and process in both learning and assessment. For many tutors, assessment is still seen as having two aims: to provide students with the results of their performance and to give them an award of intellectual or vocational competence. Yet this performative approach is too narrow for problem-based approaches where the process of learning is also viewed as important. Students here need to be enabled to assess how they learn and be equipped so that they know how to provide evidence of this learning. There is little real acknowledgement that most students today use strategic approaches to learning – many of us in higher education are idealists who expect students to enjoy learning for its own sake. While we struggle to get students excited about our subject or get them to think beyond the material presented, many of us know that most of them (who were working in a bar until midnight) just want to get through the course. If we were to acknowledge strategic approaches to learning and assessment, perhaps we could then provide something more student-centred, and negotiate assessments and design them with our students.

However, if we are to develop new or different assessments that reflect the philosophy of problem-based learning, we do need to take our students with us. It is vital to de-mystify assessment criteria and help students to become stakeholders in the assessment process. One way of doing this is to ask students to develop their own marking criteria, because they will then understand what the process of grading involves. This may appear time-consuming and something students may find hard to do, but it may lessen plagiarism and encourage honesty and personal responsibility in the team, while also helping students to perform better on other forms of assessment.

The role of the facilitator in the assessment process

There is much debate globally about the role of the facilitator as assessor, because if the team facilitator is also the assessor it tends to affect the power dynamics in problem-based learning tutorials. If assessment is undertaken, it is usually better in problem-based learning for it to be done anonymously, as in most other learning approaches. Furthermore, if assessment of the team process is to be undertaken, then this is best done by someone other than the team facilitator, since this avoids the complicated dynamic of the facilitator being seen as both co-learner and gatekeeper, which will tend to occur if a facilitator is required to assess the team that they also facilitate. As students become more familiar and experienced with problem-based learning, they become more autonomous in what they learn and how they manage their team and they then begin to see themselves as co-learners with the facilitators. For the facilitator to assess the students when the team are essentially running their own session as a collaborative, self-managed team would be destructive. Heron (1993) has argued that self-assessment is the key to encouraging students to manage their own learning and to move away from authoritarian approaches to assessment. For students to be assessed unilaterally by the facilitator would change the nature of learning in the team. Similarly, if the students are expected to evaluate facilitator capabilities and these evaluations affect the tutor's promotion prospects (as has happened in some American universities), this is also likely to cause dysfunction within the team. Any assessment that takes place as part of the team needs to be guided by the team and should be part of a collaborative learning and assessment process. Even if the facilitator uses formative assessment, students tend to rely on the facilitator and find it difficult to become independent in inquiry. In reality, it is difficult for tutors to be a peer to student team members, and when facilitators take up the role of assessors of the teams they facilitate, this tends to distort team dynamics and power relationships. If students are to be assessed on the process of learning in teams by analysing what occurs when the team meets, this is best done through peer assessment but also by using other methods, such as the 'tripartite assessment', to ensure equity in the team.

Conclusion

So we are left with a number of questions and concerns. Why is it that we assess students in the ways that we do? Why are we so focused upon outcomes but have little time for process? It seems that even when the learning process is assessed it is undertaken using Likert scales and some qualitative feedback – yet the students have commented that they value the qualitative feedback from tutors and peers more than being given grades. We need to be asking questions about how we assess a pedagogy for supercomplexity and manage the relationship between such a pedagogy and competence to practise. What is required are forms of assessment that are valued by both staff and students, which do not decontextualize the subject, are meaningful to the students and aligned to problem-based learning, whichever typology of problem-based learning is being used.

Part 4

Rhetorical Communities

9

Reconceptualizing Problem-based Learning Curricula

Introduction

This chapter examines how problem-based learning curricula are conceived and suggests that changes need to be made to how we construct such curricula. It begins by examining what is meant by curriculum, in particular the shifts that have taken place towards more mechanistic formulations of curricula. The final section considers the ways in which political change towards more authoritarian forms of leadership in universities has affected, and continues to affect, the extent to which it is possible to both design and implement problem-based learning curricula that support the student in developing independence in inquiry in any real sense.

Models, types or taxonomies?

One area that seems to be under-researched in problem-based learning is the notion of curriculum. In earlier work, I argued for models of problem-based learning that operate within a curriculum, models that some have since suggested, in conversation, should be seen as a taxonomy (Savin-Baden 2000a). The models are not, essentially, meant to be construed as being hierarchical, but instead are meant to allow those designing or who have designed curricula using problem-based learning to examine and recognize the underpinning assumptions associated with the different models, and to raise awareness that problem-based learning can be operated in a number of different ways. However, what is perhaps a fundamental omission is the examination of the place, position and construction of the curriculum in higher education in general, and how different types of curricula do and do not facilitate the introduction and maintenance of problem-based learning.

The notion of curriculum

Although we talk about the notion of and construction of a curriculum, in many ways we do not, as it were, *have* a curriculum, since it is constructed with and through our students. If then the learning intentions we place in the validation document are spoken of in terms of an abiding concern for the life-worlds of the students, then we need to examine the process of meaning construction with our subjects and disciplines, and clarify how meanings are embodied within these and in the language used by staff and students. Thus the types of questions we should be asking are: 'What does knowing mean in this context?' 'How do we create a curriculum that engages in the construction and development of knowing?' Barnett has argued:

> Interpreted broadly and correctly 'curriculum' embraces the students' engagement with the offerings put before them. But a curriculum is, in any case, a statement of what counts as knowledge in several senses ... The medium *is* the message
>
> (Barnett 1994: 45–6)

Curricula for which problem-based learning is central to the learning are in fact largely constructivist in nature because students do, to a large extent, make decisions about what counts as knowledge and knowing. What is problematic here is how such a constructivist stance can be married with benchmarking standards and the emerging audit culture in higher education. In recent years, we have seen such a shift towards accountability and transparency that the focus in many curricula is more upon outcomes and less upon learning. While the initial aims of quality assurance mechanisms, such as the Quality Assurance Agency, may have been laudable in their attempts to put teaching quality centre stage, what has occurred instead is that the process has been hijacked for other agenda. There are also other strange assumptions, such as the belief that outcomes and benchmarking standards will somehow make learning better, or will prove competence to practise or even make what is taught auditable across the same subject in different universities. Such naive assumptions pervade large areas of higher education that appear to have forgotten the maxims of Dewey about the separation of 'mind' from a direct occupation with things, which, in turn, means that there tends to be a focus on '*things* at the expense of *relations* of connections' (Dewey 1938: 167). Such separation of perceptions from judgement and attempts to define separated items of knowledge is not only resulting in students becoming strategic and competency-led learners, but also is downgrading the kind of integrated learning that helps to make connections and understand the relations between things.

The wisdom of Stenhouse has been largely ignored. He suggested that we must beware of believing that the objective model of education was the solution to larger curricular problems and argued, 'We do not *have* objectives: we choose to conceptualize our behaviour in terms of objectives – or we choose not to' (Stenhouse 1975: 71). What is interesting about the work of Stenhouse is that many of the important points he made about designing curricula have been discounted, and the result has been an increasing move towards outcome measures and performance so that students are seen as dogs who salivate rather than as people who live and work in context and in relation to each other. The importance of Stenhouse's work to problem-based learning curricula is that he distinguished between training, instruction, initiation and induction. Training is seen as the acquisition of skills, with the result that successful training is deemed as the capacity for performance. Instruction is concerned with the learning of information, so that successful instruction results in retention of information, such as a recipe for making chocolate cake. Initiation involves becoming familiar with social values and norms, so that successful initiation would be seen as the ability to not only interpret the social environment, but also to anticipate the reactions to one's actions within it. Finally, induction involves the introduction of someone into the thought system of the culture, so that successful induction would be characterized by a person's ability to develop relationships and judgements in relation to that culture – induction for some people would also be seen as education – in its broadest sense.

Stenhouse suggested that the objectives model fits well with training and also with instruction, but he tends not to deal with the issues of initiation because he argues that it tends to take place as part of a by-product of living in a community such as an English public school and thus it is part of the hidden curriculum. However, in the current climate, initiation is very much part of the process of professional education, and thus initiation is a component of undergraduate pro- fessional education, albeit covertly. Thus although Stenhouse has suggested that the main problem in applying the objectives models lies in the area of induction, I would argue that initiation is also important here. Furthermore, I would argue that in many undergraduate programmes and particularly with the increasing use of benchmarking standards, the issues of the morality of such educational practice come into question:

> . . . from a moral point of view, the emphasis on behavioural goals, despite all of the protestations to the contrary, still borders on brain washing or at least indoctrination rather than education. We begin with some notion of how we want a person to behave and then we try to manipulate him and his environ- ment so as to get him to behave as we want him to.
>
> (Kliebard 1968: 246)

The issue, then, is how we can develop curricula that allow for the moral initiation of students into the culture of the profession or discipline, while also inducting them into knowledge in ways that avoid indoctrination and promote democracy and creativity. The suggestion that 'education as induction into knowledge is successful to the extent that it makes the behavioural outcome of the students unpredictable' (Stenhouse 1975: 82) will be uncomfortable for many course leaders and managers in the current higher education system, and yet to a large extent this is what does occur in many problem-based curricula. The issue, then, is that we may have objectives, we may use Bloom's taxonomy (Bloom 1956), but although such alleged measurements exist much of what really does occur is unpredictable. The way we make it more predictable is by rigid assessment pro- cedures that encourage rote memorization and are predominantly authoritarian in nature, thus leaving the students with little option for imagination and creativity in the way that they approach the assessment. However, what would perhaps be a more moral way of designing problem-based curricula would be to embrace the unpredictability of student learning and behaviour, and acknowledge it in curriculum documents by adopting the use of learning intentions rather than learning outcomes. Thus, in practice, designing such curricula would involve adopting some of the principles of Stenhouse's process model. This would mean that the teachers' learning intentions would be specified, as would the content of the curriculum, so that the principles behind the pedagogy of the curriculum become expressed in pedagogical aims rather than measurable outcomes. What occurs then is that the curriculum becomes based upon the idea that knowledge is contested and speculative and thus although content is specified there is little, if any, disciplinary structure.

Problem-based learning curricula

The difficulty with designing curricula stems from attempts both to define clear models of problem-based curricula and to use curriculum design models that centre on content, process or outcomes. For example, when talking with a group of staff about how they would like to redesign their curricula into a problem-based format, there is rarely any discussion about their intentions as teachers or the experiences that they would like students to have. More often the arguments centre on the content to be covered, the order in which it should be covered and how much time each discipline is going to be allowed to have, so that there is an underlying sense that the greater the length of time given to the particular discipline, subject or topic, the more it is valued. What is missing here is a concern for the learner and the learning, so that the impression is one of either training students for a profession or instructing them so that they somehow retain the knowledge we as tutors feel is important. There is little sense of education as induction and this has resulted in a focus on curriculum models and tips on designing problem-based programmes that are behaviourally focused.

However, first let us explore the issue of defining clear problem-based curriculum models. There have been a number of discussions about types of problem-based learning, the most basic being that there are two types: the pure model and the hybrid model. The argument is that either the whole curriculum is problem-based and is modelled on the McMaster version of problem-based learning, whereby students meet in small teams and do not receive lectures or tutorials, or it is the hybrid model, which is usually defined by the inclusion of fixed resources sessions, such as lectures and tutorials, which are designed to support students. Lectures may be timetabled in advance or may be requested by the students at various points in the module or programme. The so-called pure model is also often termed the Medical School Model and is invariably defined as necessarily having a dedicated facilitator for small teams of eight to ten students, being student-centred and being seen to be a good choice for highly motivated experienced learners in small cohorts (see, for example, Duch *et al.* 2001). The difficulty with this notion of there only being two types – a pure model and a hybrid model – is that given the current number of forms of problem-based learning in existence, is it possible to distinguish whether a model is hybrid or not?

In more recent years, a series of other definitions have come to the fore, such as the floating facilitator model, the peer facilitator model and the student-led model. The floating facilitator model largely resembles what has formerly been called small-group teaching and comprises students working in teams of four in the same classroom around problem scenarios supplied by the tutor. The tutor moves from team to team answering questions and at times supplying mini lectures and at the end of the session a whole-class discussion occurs. This approach would seem to have more in common with both guided discovery approaches and problem-solving learning rather than the aims of problem-based learning, since it is largely teacher-led and teacher-centred and students have little real opportunity to work out their own learning needs and to be independent inquirers.

The peer facilitator model appears to imply that members of the problem-based learning team take it in turn to facilitate the session; however, this is not what is usually meant by this model, certainly in the USA (see, for example, Duch *et al.* 2001). Instead, advanced undergraduates serve as facilitators by helping to monitor team progress and dynamics and they are expected to serve as role models for students new to problem-based learning. In the USA, such facilitators tend to be either paid for their services or given modular credits. However, it is in the student-led model that team members facilitate their own sessions. This is often used where there are large cohorts of students and there are not enough staff to facilitate the team. In some cases, it is used when the teams have been working together for some time (over six months) and it is deemed, by both the team and the existing facilitator, to be a beneficial learning experience for the students to facilitate themselves. Taylor (1997) has documented an effective example of this, whereby social work students undertaking a two-year diploma in social work have largely facilitated their own teams in the final six months of their programme.

The structure and process of curriculum design

If we are to consider ways of designing a problem-based component of a course, it is important to begin by examining what it is that we want students to learn, and then using this as the design framework for the learning intentions and problem scenarios. The problem scenarios then become the central component of each module, as in Fig. 9.1, so that lectures, seminars or skill laboratories can feed into them to inform students at the appropriate time, rather than the central components being great chunks of subject-based knowledge delivered as lectures. Designing a curriculum can begin with a single module being constructed in a way that promotes problem-based learning. For example, a twelve-week module could be designed whereby the problem scenarios match the learning intentions of the module. The other teaching methods (lectures, tutorials, laboratory sessions) support the scenarios and provide resources for students.

It would appear, then, that although there are different types of problem-based learning in operation and different models of facilitation, perhaps the most

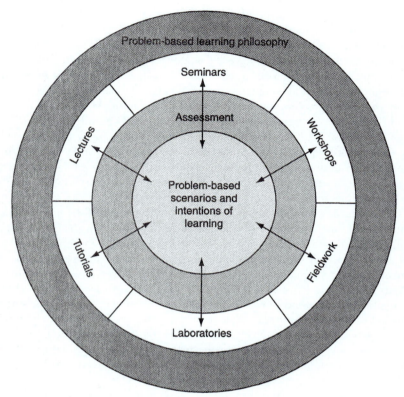

Figure 9.1   A model of problem-based learning curriculum design.

important question that needs to be asked is about the broader curriculum picture and how that is impacting upon the type of problem-based learning taken up, rather than attempting to decontextualize the type of problem-based learning from the curriculum itself. However, what I have suggested in terms of the twelve-week module is a mechanistic structure of problem-based learning decontextualized from a curriculum that offers a means of implementing problem-based learning into a module. Little real account has been taken of the complexities involved, such as the level of the course or the capabilities and processes involved. Yet despite this being a somewhat mechanistic structure, there is congruence between the philosophy of problem-based learning as an approach to learning and the process models suggested by Stenhouse (1975).

Stenhouse believed that the teacher should cast himself as a learner, as someone who has, and continues to develop, a philosophical understanding of his subject. Furthermore, the teacher should be able to understand the interrelationship of his subject to the wider social and political context and, following this, he should be able to develop the pedagogical aims of the course. What Stenhouse argued for was that as teachers or indeed facilitators of problem-based learning, we should take a critical stance towards our subject. We need to be researchers of our subjects so that the development of a curriculum can be grounded in the worlds of both teaching and research. Facilitators in the study I undertook (Savin-Baden 2000b: Ch. 4) often spoke of themselves as learners, as part of a learning team and as people who had been stimulated, through problem-based learning, to reconsider their view of learning, teaching and the nature of knowledge. What is of interest here is that such staff had already designed the curriculum and then come to realize the importance of a process model of learning. The consequence was that when these staff subsequently redesigned the problem-based curriculum some five years later, they were starting from a different pedagogical position (even though, because of the nature of curriculum design in UK universities, they were still expected to design the curriculum using objectives). The result is that from pedagogical aims the teacher is able to clarify the content of the course but also then consider their role in this process and their learning intentions – (or, as Peters (1959: 89–90) termed them, 'principles of procedure').

The curriculum, then, is designed with some notion of what is to be included but with the realization that knowledge must be speculative and contested. However, this raises the difficulty of whether in fact disciplinary knowledge exists, and how the notion of learning in particular disciplinary areas at a university is to be managed. In many problem-based learning programmes, this too has become an issue. Recently, this has promoted the use of problem-based learning in inter-professional education in health because of the similarities between what students are learning in physiotherapy compared with radiography, and in engineering compared with physics. It could be argued that this is a cost-cutting exercise in some universities, but certainly in many there is a sense that the pedagogical overlap between such professions needs to be correlated much more effectively than previously, so that it will not only benefit the student and the profession for which they are being educated but also wider society. However, there are other curriculum models that are in operation and others that are philosophical ideas that have yet to be played out in practice (Barnett 2000a,b). What is needed is a review of the different models of curricula and an examination of the ways in which problem-based learning might be used in each of these, along with the impact it is likely to have on student learning.

New managerialism and the curriculum

The development of graduate certificates and diplomas in teaching for university lecturers in the UK has prompted an increasing focus on the ways in which curricula are designed. This has occurred against the backdrop of the growing importance of the Staff and Educational Development Association (SEDA) in the late 1970s and the subsequent development of the Institute of Learning and Teaching (ILT) in the late 1990s. The ILT is an institution that accredits programmes that have been set up to train and establish lecturers teaching effectiveness, formed as a result of recommendations by the Dearing Report into Higher Education (NCIHE 1997). Yet despite such initiatives, there has been little in-depth discussion about what counts as curriculum within institutions and some of the difficulties appear to relate to the power and control exerted by university leaders. There has been a shift away from 'management' in universities towards a notion of leadership that seems to have adopted the values of commerce and industry. Yet the notion of leadership learning suggested by Middlehurst (1995), whereby leadership and leadership development included learning and understanding the art of leadership as well as learning to act as a leader, has largely been ignored. The underpinning concern here is in an active process of engagement with being a leader physically, emotionally and intellectually. These values and strategies appeared to fit well within higher education, yet now what has been adopted instead are the values of enterprise and value-added with little real understanding of what the latter actually means for staff or students. The new controlling and directive leadership where the vice-chancellor holds all the purse strings and gives little real power to his pro-vice-chancellors seems to be one that is becoming more common. Such leadership to some extent reflects the politics in the UK and the USA, where increased control by the leaders has resulted in greater control over almost every area of public life. University leadership has left behind any notion of organizational learning and the development of autonomy as a component of academic life, and instead we see the continuing rise of the accountability culture. The result is that the main role of leadership in many universities is seen by staff as the ability to manage funds, ensure quality and obtain funds with less and less of an emphasis on the management of innovation and change. Pritchard recently suggested that current managerial practice within UK universities could be understood as:

- managed by a manager, rather than administered by an elected representative;
- customer- rather than student-focused;
- reviewed by quality assurance audit rather than by peer review;
- corporately rather than professionally orientated;
- strategically rather than tactically focused.

(Pritchard 2000:198)

This new brand of leadership has resulted not only in an increasingly fragmented culture in higher education, as Usher and Edwards (1994) have suggested, but a move back to modernity styles of management in higher education. This seems to have begun in the 1990s with modularization, but the further unitizing of learning that has occurred as a result of Qualtiy Assurance Agency (QAA) procedures and some of the negative consequences of the professionalization of teaching, such as the hints-and-tips culture and the uncritical induction of (new) staff into particular kinds of teaching techniques, has meant that learning has become compartmentalized into training and instruction. The result is increased separation between disciplines and greater separation between learning and assessment. This has occurred because of the unintended side-effects of the QAA categories, but also because of the way in which learning is divided up into segments and then assessed. Many students now see learning at universities as something that is largely separate from, rather than integral to, their lives – even in curricula that provide education for the professions. The result of this is that

university leaders feel duty bound to ensure that their university curricula con-
form to given criteria, standards and values. The consequence is that institutional
learning and teaching strategies are used to impose structures that may not fit
across all disciplines and subjects. Some years ago, I was running a study day at
a university where staff wanted to implement problem-based learning in their
programmes. Although the leadership at the university espoused the value of
innovative and integrative forms of learning, such as problem-based learning, the
system that had been imposed made it difficult to develop programmes that
supported integrated experiences of learning for students. A geography lecturer
explained how the new teaching dean had imposed a new structure whereby all
modules had to have the same number of credit points, extend over the same
number of weeks and be assessed within the same time frame. Modules could not
be joined together, two modules could not be assessed with one piece of work, and
modules could not take place outside the semester system. The problem for him
was how he was going to standardize his geography field trip to Switzerland
each summer that lasted for three weeks and which informed both the learning
and assessment that occurred in other modules. In the same session, a lecturer in
midwifery also pointed out that the imposition of undergraduate generic research
modules at given points in the curriculum interrupted the practice component of
the programme, were not related in any way to student learning about research in
midwifery, and that students did not understand why they were doing such modules
when all the other modules in the problem-based learning undergraduate programme seemed to fit together except these.

A colleague from a different university also complained that it was almost
impossible to implement problem-based learning that integrated learning
across the disciplines because she, as a lecturer in psychology, had to teach pure
psychology to the nursing students because no-one but psychologists were allowed
to teach that subject at her university and the same applied to other applied
sciences. Such difficulties are not uncommon and it seems that there has been
little realization that such strategies not only devalue the notion of disciplinary
knowledge and understanding, but also stifle the development of creative and
imaginative curricula.

Curricula for whom?

There are universities worldwide, perhaps more accurately departments within
universities, who are embracing what Hannan and Silver (2000) have termed 'a
culture of change'. What they mean is that such universities subscribe to the notion
of change in a way that enables them to respond both flexibly and rapidly to new
demands, yet underpinning this is only a partial enthusiasm for what is new, since
what is at issue at a more basic level is the fear of otherwise losing out to competitors who may gain ground. Thus innovations such as problem-based learning
are often used as a means to develop curricula, onto which it is then possible to
add other political agenda such as inter-professional education, bids for improving
teaching and collaborative bids with competitors. The number of submissions

to the Teaching Quality Enhancement Fund in the UK in 2002 that included problem-based learning was considerably higher than in previous years. This indicates not only the growing use of problem-based learning, but also the realization that there is now money to be had for changing teaching practices. Learning, it seems, is finally becoming big business. Yet at the heart of all this should be students and their development but there is confusion here. Approaches such as problem-based learning are designed to embrace the notion of inducting the students into knowledge while also helping them to own their own learning and develop independence in inquiry. There is an expectation that problem-based learning can not only subsume the values of liberal education (that it is the kind of education where students are encouraged to have virtually unrestricted access to knowledge and that knowledge is to be valued for its own sake), but also equip students for the new age of information and global competition. Yet is the position more sinister than that? It has been suggested that current notions of competence embrace student-centred learning, because by encouraging students to take control over their learning they will become competent members of the workforce: 'In being incorporated into this discourse, self discipline through self control and competent performance reconfigures the need for direct control of the work force' (Usher and Edwards 1994: 111).

Usher and Edwards have argued that despite the intensification of labour processes in increasing productivity, at the same time there has been a weakening of traditional authoritarian management practices. Yet I would argue that this shift may in fact be largely superficial – it may be that the practices are visible but in fact new managerialism practices do incorporate many of the earlier authoritarian ones. New managerialism is an attempt to understand and delineate the managerial techniques usually associated with businesses onto public sector and voluntary organizations. The characteristics that emerge when new managerialism is in operation are marketization, particularly of public services, the encouragement of competition between employees, the redefinition of higher education as a commodity providing service, an increase of the auditing and monitoring of professional work, and the monitoring of efficiency and effectiveness through the measurement of outcomes and individual staff performances (Deem 1998; Trowler 1998). In particular, these can be seen in the ideals of human resource management, whereby self-discipline and self-management are used to patrol the workforce, but such control is hidden behind a language of competence and a humanistic stance so that 'the organisation as a whole becomes subject to greater surveillance, articulated through a discourse of accountability' (Usher and Edwards 1994: 113). What is important, then, in planning and designing problem-based curricula will be the acknowledgement of these conflicting but interrelated forces, so that not only is this marketization of problem-based learning addressed, but also are the blurring of boundaries between previously distinct categories of practice and systems of values (Bernstein 1971).

Conclusion

This chapter has considered some of the overarching difficulties inherent in constructing problem-based curricula at a time when higher education would seem to be in a continuous state of revolution. For many teachers in higher education, particularly those involved in the education of students for the professions, there is an increasing blurring of the divide between higher education and practice and, in some cases, the public and private sector. Such changes and challenges are influencing curriculum design. Furthermore, the values underpinning the design and development of problem-based learning curricula are becoming increasingly complex, as staff are expected to meet multiple agendas and a diversity of concerns raised by customers, leaders, politicians and the public and private sector. The idea that curricula need to be more imaginative is an issue that has been discussed in detail in the early 2000s within UK higher education, and in the next chapter the relationship between these new curriculum models and problem-based learning will be explored.

10

Facilitating Learning Through Problem-based Curricula

Introduction

Learning, facilitation and problem-based learning are all terms and ideals that we could deconstruct and argue about. To some extent, the debates about all of these have been discussed in earlier chapters. This chapter examines what it means to facilitate learning on problem-based learning courses. This is not done by using particular techniques to make learning better for students or using ways to re-examine learning, but instead by exploring the whole issue around curriculum-making in the organizational context of higher education and by examining what this might mean for those wanting to, and continuing to, implement problem-based learning. It will also examine the impact of implementing wide-scale problem-based learning in the higher education sector and explore the possibilities for facilitating different kinds of problem-based learning curricula in different kinds of institutional settings.

Generic or imaginative curricula structures?

There has been little discussion recently about whether it would be possible to have different curricula designs for different subjects and disciplines. In the problem-based learning community, the discussions largely centre on how to manage this form of learning within the constraints of the curriculum, and which subversive ways can be used to circumvent the often stringent and tightly bound modular structures. At the same time, questions concerning problem-based learning, both in workshops and conferences, arise about whether facilitating such learning is any different from the way in which young children are engaged in learning through play and exploration. Some staff will argue that there is little difference and that if we build on what children learned early in life, there would be little conflict for students between problem-based learning and learning in schools. A further argument in the problem-based learning community is about the way in which the school system generally rewards little other than grade-based achievement. Another

view is that it is often taken for granted both at school and at university that students
know a considerable amount before they arrive, and then they are informed that
their knowing is worth relatively little, in an academic sense. The most recent
discussions, in the UK at least, are about whether problem-based learning is not
only the latest fashion but also a political tool to make sure that tutors comply with
the wishes of those in the corridors of power. Yet it would appear that most people
who are implementing problem-based learning are doing so because they feel it is a
form of learning that is beneficial for all stakeholders, and not because someone in
the vice-chancellor's office has told them to do so. However, it might be that most of
the growth in problem-based learning is at the lower end of the hierarchy and that:

> Those at the top, or near the top, of this hierarchy may maintain their position
> more by attracting and holding key academic stars than by changing their
> pedagogic discourse according to the exigencies of the market . . . On the
> other hand, those institutions which are much less fortunate in their position in
> the stratification . . . Will be more concerned with the marketing possibilities
> of their pedagogic discourse.
>
> (Bernstein 1996: 74)

Perhaps what we are seeing is that those at the top need not push problem-based
learning because they want to hold on to their stars. Meanwhile those at the bottom
are being encouraged, or even financially supported, in developing a pedagogic
discourse, in the form of problem-based learning, which is seen to be more market-
able to students and in particular to the world of work. Barnett, too, has argued
that the power, influence and hierarchical position of the institution affect the type
of curriculum on offer. He has suggested that there are multiple forces competing
for influence on the contemporary curriculum, from the State, the labour market,
knowledge fields and institutions. Drawing on Bernstein, Barnett has argued that
curricula may be either 'inward-looking, reflecting a project of introjection where
they are largely the outcome of academic influence', or 'outward looking, reflecting
a project of projection, where they are subject to external influences' (Barnett
2000b: 263–4). Barnett predicts that at the macro-level (state and institutional
policy), change will be in the direction of projection and from insulated singulars
towards increasingly multi- or inter-disciplinary regions. Yet despite the multiple
claims from outside the academe, he suggested that 'the discipline (or knowledge
field) constitutes the largest claim on the identity of academics' (p. 264) and, consequently, the micro-level of actual curricular changes will reflect both the extent to
which disciplines within institutions are yielding their insularity and the changes
within disciplinary fields of inquiry. Thus Barnett believes that change will largely
depend upon the relative strength of institutions against that of their constituent
disciplines, and the positioning of individual institutions within the higher education system. What is interesting about this argument is Barnett's belief that disciplinary identities will necessarily prevail over performativity where institutions are
powerfully positioned in the national hierarchy of universities.

Yet the real struggles for those in the problem-based learning community seem to
be associated more often with the demands of curriculum-making, difficulties with
the restrictions imposed within university systems and boundaries imposed by some

disciplines. As I discussed in Chapter 9, modularization is a constant difficulty. The early arguments for modularization were about increasing student choice and making what was taught more lucid than in former years. It could be argued that modularization encouraged university lecturers to make explicit their learning and teaching practices and what was being taught in their modules and this, in many cases, improved the quality of student learning. Yet I would argue that, although modularization was a step in the direction of quality, that instead of moving beyond it we have become locked into debates about types and lengths and assessment of modules rather than reconceptualizing curricula. Recent research has shown that in one cohort students tended to read more and work towards the modular objectives and assessment if the modules were short (about ten weeks), while in longer modules they did little background reading and only went to the library to search for information just before the modular assessment was due (McKenna 2002). Although this research has stimulated debate about curriculum design, assessment and students' motivation, it also points up that students appear to be so overwhelmed by the diversity of modules, the amount of assessment and the expectation of different tutors, that they have little time for debate, reflection and taking a stance towards their learning, particularly in short modules. For many students, getting a degree is about jumping modular hurdles of different heights and lengths, with little sense of an overall fusion between them. If we are not only to improve the student experience but also encourage students to value process and develop critical thought, we need to develop imaginative possibilities for learning. The starting point for this is in redesigning all our curricula, not just those that are problem-based, so that we move beyond modularization towards something that centres not just on outcomes but also intentions, and thus helps students to value the process and the product of learning. Many staff complain that the curricula on which they teach are assessment-driven and that students only focus on the assessment. At a very basic level, this is because curricula are behavioural. Curricula have objectives, assessment is the focus and the reward and students inevitably respond like rats in a maze – but are rarely as well fed. The only real way we can move students away from being assessment-focused is to redesign curricula so that they are more imaginative.

Broadly speaking, it is possible to divide understandings about curriculum design into three categories: those that focus on structure, those that emphasize process and those that attempt to do both. The reasons for the emphasis tend to be con-textual in nature, usually related to the type of university, its view of academic freedom and the way in which knowledge is controlled and patrolled within the discipline or subject area. Polytechnics worldwide, and the UK post-1992 uni-versities, tend to focus highly on structural design that fits with both the expectation of the Quality Assurance Agency and the subject and professional benchmarking criteria. There is becoming a sense that 'more of the same' is better and thus if all programmes are standardized this will mean that the quality of courses will be better. In fact, what is likely to occur is that standards may look the same but the quality will vary. If benchmarking or quality assurance serve to help staff to high-light current practice and learn from one another, then this can be a stimulating and imaginative process, but in the main this does not seem to be the case. It appears that benchmarking is time-consuming and labour-intensive and that so far little real account seems to have been taken of the different professional and university cultures. There needs to be a recognition that benchmarking *can* be a form of intuitional learning, but only if a critical stance is taken towards the standards that have been created. In the process of curriculum design, it seems that the intuitional and professional context of learning is not often taken into account and we need to acknowledge that what works in some professions, institutions and countries may not be desired or required elsewhere.

It has been suggested that curriculum design in higher education in the past tended to lie at the artistic end of the spectrum and that there has been a shift towards adopting a more scientific approach to this process (Jackson and Shaw 2002). The result, Jackson and Shaw suggest, is 'The use of conceptual knowledge and visual knowledge representations in curriculum making is a manifestation of a more scientific approach to being a teacher'. It is not clear what Jackson and Shaw mean by 'scientific', but what is evident from their paper is that the debate about what counts as a curriculum and what it might look like has promoted much interesting debate in the UK. Yet what seems to have occurred through this fascinating discussion process is the production of a plethora of diagrams that are deemed to represent different forms, and possibly even taxonomies, of curricula. What appears to be at issue here is whether such diagrams are useful in designing curricula and, in particular here, problem-based ones. Previously, universities with a greater degree of autonomy and academic freedom tended to focus on curriculum design not as an art or a science, but as a process of induction into knowledge that reflected the discipline. However, several models have been high-lighted through the Imaginative Curriculum Project (Jackson and Shaw 2002) that appear to bring together both structure and process, including the Constructive Alignment model (Biggs 1999), the Complexity model (Barnett 2000b; Barnett and Coates 2002) and the Capability model (Stephenson 2002), which I shall call group intentional models.

Structural design models

Structural design models tend to be product-orientated and are consequently market-guided or market-led. What is common to these models of curriculum design is that they are structured and bounded by modularity, but the relationship between the modules varies depending upon the type of model. Many of these curricula are seen as having a product to sell and thus students are seen as customers who will choose to buy the product. Students as consumers must receive a quick response if they complain and the course must be adapted according to the market demands and consumer preferences. Much of what occurs in these programmes in terms of the market and the consumer is kept under wraps, and few academics would admit to the (rapid) changes that are made in response to students' demands. However, with the advent of performance-related pay and students' evaluation increasingly being used to inform curriculum production, structural design that is consumer-led is likely to increase significantly in the years ahead. What we see currently are three particular types of structural design models: serviced modular curricula, notional modular curricula and genuine modular curricula.

Serviced modular curricula

These curricula tend to be disparate and many students have difficulty in making connections not only across modules but also within them. The curricula are modular, designed using behavioural objectives and are usually those where students are being educated for the professions. Thus knowledge is not exclusive to the profession but instead is drawn from a number of disciplinary areas and sub-sumed into the curriculum. What happens is that a curriculum is designed in, for example, business studies or social work, and both of these curricula require that students study law and psychology. Instead of these subjects being taught in the context of business studies or social work, by staff who have worked and researched in those fields, belong to the department and teach students at other times, they are serviced by academics from law and psychology. Students are thus taught law and psychology in a way that is decontextualized from their subject. The information that is taught is rarely applied to practice and students find it difficult to understand how it is related to other learning that has occurred in different modules. The reason for taking this route both in the UK and in Australia appears to be the need for particular disciplinary areas to hold on to the ground that, by discipline, has always been theirs. The university system supports this and thus 'applied' courses are serviced by the 'purer' disciplines. A more recent trend seems to be a different form of servicing. What occurs here is that a large research methods team is created from interested parties across the university. This team teach large groups of students from a variety of disciplines how to undertake research at undergraduate or pre-registration level. Again there is relatively little application to the specific area for which the student is studying and, as a result, students tend to see little point in both the module and in doing research. These serviced modular curricula seem to be a way of knowledge management and a means of keeping academics employed in disciplines where student numbers are decreasing while those in applied subjects are increasing. Yet students' experience of these modules appears to be fragmented and deleterious.

Notional modular curricula

Many of the notional modular curricula can be found in degrees where students are being educated for the professions. What occurs here is that the curricula is, to all intents and purposes, modular and students, it is alleged, are able to take other modules from other programmes. Furthermore, students from other degrees can take a module in, for example, the accountancy, surveying or physiotherapy degree. However, in practice, the modules are so well integrated and in most cases built so that most are foundational either to earlier modules or to the entry requirement, that it is almost impossible to take a module from such a curriculum. Here those who have designed the curriculum have been careful to highlight where students can insert a module from other areas and point out which modules can be taken by students from other programmes, but in fact this is unlikely to happen and the timetables are so intertwined that it is not actually possible for a physics student to undertake the communication skills module in the occupational therapy degree.

Genuine modular curricula

There are few genuine modular curricula in the UK, whereas there are many more in a variety of forms in the USA. In the USA, students can choose to take a degree which encompasses a range of subjects and a wide variety of modules. In the UK, this is broadly possible in some areas of business studies, English and environmental science, but in few other disciplinary areas. The advantage for students is that they do have genuine choice about the subjects they study and, in many cases, the order in which they can take them. However, the disadvantage is that for many, gaining a degree becomes a very fragmented experience, and because students take many varied modules there is little real sense of a cohesive structure or dialogic learning experience for them. For staff, teaching on this kind of curriculum is generally unsatisfactory, because it tends to be isolating, they rarely come to know their students and there is little real sense of inducting the students into their discipline.

Process design models

In process design models, the notion of getting students to learn is central but how this is conceived and played out is different in each one of the three on offer: the content model, the learning model and the process model. Many of the process models are utopian in their stance and as a result there may be difficulty with such models for students whose focus is on high grades, or who find it problematic to articulate their approach(es) to learning. However, this would not be the case with the content model.

Content model

The focus in curricula that adopt the content model is on ways of maximizing the knowledge transferred to students. Knowledge is seen as propositional and thus the emphasis in these curricula is on mode 1 knowledge, knowledge produced in the academe, separate from its use (Gibbons *et al.*, 1994). Staff here see their role as ensuring students cover the content that they provide and ask them to read, so that they can demonstrate their knowledge through examinations. In some programmes, students are encouraged to critique the knowledge put before them, but in the main they are required to learn a different body of knowledge at each level of the programme, depending how difficult the knowledge is perceived to be by the staff. Within this model, staff tend to believe that some knowledge is necessarily foundational to other knowledge and that students need to cover pillar-type 'basic concepts' before moving on (Kandlbinder and Maufette 2001; see also Chapter 4). The strong disciplinary nature of these subjects and the way knowledge is bounded tends to mean that the content model is seen at the higher end of the hierarchy, characterized by the production of mode 1 knowledge in subjects such as the pure sciences.

Learning model

In this model, the overarching dimension of the curriculum is in creating conditions for students to learn. This could include Rogerian principles (Rogers 1983), but more often the tendency is to take up the cognitive psychology position. In the past, the focus was on seeking to provide a curriculum in which the achievement of the objective was paramount and what could be counted or observed was recognized as learning. The assumption was that learning and behaviour could be measured through discrete or observable behaviour, and that staff marking examinations were objective and reliable (in both senses). However, the shift in recent years has been towards a more cognitive than behavioural perspective. Although many curricula are still written in behavioural terms, with approaches to assessment also being behavioural, the emphasis is now largely on human thinking and the study of memory. The curriculum would then, in this instance, focus on ways of maximizing the use of memory and developing expertise in the students. Understanding (that has taken place through learning) is defined in terms of the coherent organization of concepts and examples, exemplified by the conception of deep approaches to learning. The focus on such curricula is on finding ways of helping students to develop a deep approach. Yet, as Haggis (2002) has argued, there does appear to be some conflict around the notion of developing a deep approach, in that approaches are difficult to change and in many instances surface approaches can result in very successful learning. What is important though, in the learning models of curriculum design, is the emphasis on context, practice and the argument that problem-solving is not a generic skill but is context-dependent. Thus in these curricula there is a concentration on strategies to maximize practice and teaching approaches that enhance transfer.

Learning models of curriculum design are seen in a variety of contexts but are often prevalent in medicine, law and dentistry. Here the focus is on the application of propositional knowledge to a practice context. What is problematic is that it is the students who are expected to do the applying and transferring, often with relatively little help from staff. Learning models emphasize memory and recall, centre upon becoming expert and often use projects and simulations to promote transfer.

Process model

The focus in these modules is on specific approaches that are designed to help students to learn. This is not about creating learning conditions for students, but approaches that are designed to engage the students in 'learning for the whole person' (Heron 1993). Holistic learning, Heron has argued, can be about living and learning in the world or learning in the classroom. The distinction he made was between being involved in learning as a subject as opposed to learning to become a whole person. For the most part, the process model in higher education is about the involvement of the self in learning about a subject. Heron's notion of learning to become a whole person, while enticing, would not seem to be a possibility in the current outcomes-driven system in the UK – or anywhere else. Other process models such as those suggested by Knight (2002) and that practised at Alverno College would seem to be more realistic. The focus at Alverno College, USA, is in developing students' capabilities, giving feedback and finding appropriate assessment. The curriculum is ability-based and because of this students must be able to understand and utilize the assessment criteria effectively so that they can self- and peer-assess. Although it is a small college, with small class sizes and more resources than most UK institutions, the focus on built-in standards, equipping students for assessment and promoting cooperative and peer approaches for learning and staff development is something from which we could learn.

Knight's process approach to curriculum design is one that he has suggested will support complex learning, which is derived from complexity theory:

> Complexity theories, of which explanations of quantum phenomena are a subset, say that the natural world is, in the main, different. They replace the specific certainties of classical mechanics with probabilistic statements about what is likely to happen in groups. They add that the same starting conditions can lead to different outcomes at different times, while different starting conditions can lead to the same outcome, a point well grasped by modern researchers into school effectiveness.
>
> (Knight 2002)

What Knight is arguing for is the design of outcomes, but not ones that are predictable. Students should be able to defend their achievements and thus the assessment system will need to be designed to recognize this and to give responsive feedback. Knight's model could be classed as being intentional in that it sits at the borders of intentional and process models, but his arguments for quality management are at odds with the rest of his argument. Furthermore, although he argues for rational curriculum planning, he does not offer a means of using the model. It may be possible to use it in postgraduate courses, counselling degrees or postgraduate certificates in learning and teaching.

Intentional design models

These models are those with the initial position that the teacher begins by developing the pedagogical aims of the course and from these she clarifies the content of the course. However, what is important here is that the teacher considers her role in this process and her learning intentions. In such curricula, what students learn is somewhat unpredictable and the view is taken that knowledge is seen as being constructed by the students in relation to the pedagogical aims of the teacher. Notions of both knowledge and curriculum, therefore, become contested ground and both staff and students evaluate personal knowledge and propositional knowledge in the process of curriculum construction. Curriculum construction is thus an active, interrupted and often fragmented process. Within such construction, the stances and identities of students and staff are, however, still recognized.

Constructively aligned model

The constructive alignment model proposed by Biggs (1999) has all the hallmarks of an intentional model, but in fact there are difficulties with this model.

> Constructive alignment starts with the notion that the learner constructs his or her own learning through relevant learning activities. The teacher's job is to broker a learning environment that supports the learning activities appropriate to achieving the desired learning outcomes. The key is that all the components in the teaching system, the curriculum and its intended outcomes, the teaching methods used, the assessment tasks are aligned to each other. All are tuned to learning activities addressed in the intended outcomes. The learner finds it difficult to escape without learning.
>
> (Biggs 2002)

What is problematic here is Biggs' notion of constructivism, as I argued earlier, but in particular here that the learner is essentially trapped into learning. This is contrary to understandings of constructivism and a somewhat sinister approach to the management of students. At times what Biggs appears to be arguing for is some form of covert behaviourism, by which students are manipulated into a position of undertaking activities that will necessarily make them take up a deep approach. He impales himself further with his own argument when he states that a student who is not engaging 'in terms of what is properly required' (Biggs 1999: 14) can subsequently graduate with a first-class honours degree in psychology. A further difficulty is his reliance on cognitive psychology and the resultant Structure of the Observed Learning Outcome (SOLO) taxonomy that, while interesting and useful, is at odds with constructivism. If this model was implemented in a constructivist framework, as opposed to one embedded in cognitive psychology, it would enable a coalition to be made between problem-based learning and constructive alignment forms of curriculum design. The current model would seem intentional, but the practices Biggs has suggested do not fit well with either constructivism or problem-based learning.

The capability model

The Capability Envelope has been proposed by Stephenson (2002) and is a curriculum model that is designed to help students to be equipped for multiple settings and situations, both predictable and unpredictable. He has suggested that students should be enabled to design and manage their own strategic educational development. For Stephenson, student opportunities for learning are restricted if staff define the purpose, content and the direction of learning, and close down opportunities for students to become equipped to deal with ambiguous situations and an unpredictable future. The framework he suggests is a staged approach that is part of the overall curriculum but envelops content:

> The Envelope begins with an **Exploration Stage** in which students are helped to plan and negotiate approval for their programmes of study; continues with a **Progress Review Stage** running through the main study phase, in which students are helped to monitor and review their progress; and ends with a **Demonstration Stage** in which students show what they have learnt through the application of their learning to real situations relevant to their intended career.

> (Stephenson 2002)

The design is such that the stages build upon one another and it is thus expected that this will offer the learner a coherent structure to their learning. It would appear that the basis for the model is the development of life-long learning in students, and as such it fits and overlaps with many of the stages involved in problem-based learning. It would also seem to fit with mode 2 knowledge, applied forms of knowledge that, in this case, may be constructed by students in the academe but which are designed for use in practice. Furthermore, as students are asked to be involved in the planning and implementing of their learning, self-direction and autonomy are encouraged through this capability model. However, what is not clear is the way in which this is related to other modules, or whether in fact this is a framework that students are expected to manage for themselves. What seems to be occurring in this model is that although the capabilities are wrapped around content, it is difficult to see how integration occurs. If this is the case, then it would have some of the same problems as multi-inclusion curricula (Savin-Baden 2000a), whereby key skills are bolted on and students struggle to understand the relationship between content and skills, when in fact both capabilities and skills need to be seen as integral to the learning content, not separate from it.

Complexity model

Although Barnett and Coates (2002) have not termed it as such, I would argue here that what they are proposing is a complexity model, since it reflects the earlier work of Barnett on supercomplexity. The model takes the notion of curriculum a stage further and seeks to embed Barnett's theorizing in a view of curriculum that reflects the fragmented world of both the learners and the curriculum designers. Of the many models here, this one appears to have one of the better fits for problem-based learning for critical contestability.

The proposed model is based on an understanding of modern curricula as an educational project forming identities founded in three domains: those of knowledge, action and self. The 'knowledge' domain refers to the discipline-specific competences. The 'action' domain includes those competences acquired through 'doing', such as an oral presentation in art history. The 'self' domain develops an educational identity in relation to the subject areas. What Barnett and Coates suggest is that the weight of each of the three domains varies across curricula, that the domains may be integrated or held separate (but it is not entirely clear how this works) and, finally, curricular changes tend to be dominated by epistemological differences in the disciplines. What this means in practice is that:

> The curricula in science and technology courses are heavily weighted towards the knowledge domain. The domains are held separate (there is little or no integration between the domains). The arts and humanities curricula are also heavily weighted by the knowledge domain, but here there is more integration with the self domain. In the professional subject areas, there is a high degree of integration across the three domains.
>
> (Barnett and Coates 2002)

While it would seem to be the model with the best fit for problem-based learning for critical contestability across all disciplines, two important questions are not dealt with in this curriculum framework. The first is the issue of assessment: How do we assess a pedagogy for supercomplexity? The second is how we manage the relationship between a pedagogy for supercomplexity and competence to practise. For this model to work in practice, these questions would need to be addressed.

Distinct problem-based learning curricula for different institutional settings?

If we are to juxtapose these different curricula frameworks with the different models of problem-based learning discussed earlier (Chapter 1), there are endless possibilities as can be seen in Table 10.1. Yet there are still a few recurring concerns about the implementation of problem-based learning wholesale within universities. The global picture indicates that there are pockets of implementation in some universities, such as the sciences at the University of Delaware in the USA and the Department of Health and Social Care at University of Teesside in the UK. Others have a few problem-based learning modules scattered throughout the institution, whereas others have complete programmes that are problem-based, such as Salford University in the UK, McMaster University in Canada, the University of Maastricht in the Netherlands and Newcastle University in Australia. However, what is common to all of these is that they feel students require variety and diversity in learning, that staff need to be clear about the model of problem-based learning they are adopting and the way that fits with the overall university curricula framework, and that the resource implications have to be carefully considered. Greenley (2002) explored the use of problem-based learning in nurse education in the UK. She sought to understand the impact of problem-based learning on library use and how the experience of UK librarians in universities where problem-based learning was being utilized related to that documented in the literature. She found that 56 per cent of nursing programmes in the UK were using problem-based learning in some way. Although 61 per cent of these had noted a change in library usage, she found that this figure dropped to 34 per cent when only the respondents with courses using a 'wholly problem-based learning track' were considered. What was of interest was that library staff noted a change in enquiries, students wanting facilitation in finding information, and librarians often found it difficult to know how much guidance to offer students in these programmes.

However, the problems are not just those of the UK. Although South Africa is leading the world in its management of discrimination and societal transformation, the academic community is struggling with a different kind of curriculum restructuring. Moore has used the argument of UK colleagues (Moore and Young 2001) to suggest that the movement for change in South Africa is exerting pressure on both the modes of knowledge production and the forms of curriculum organization that are possible. The push towards integration that is occurring is resulting in what would seem to be a performative slide as a result of 'increasing connectivity between disciplines, between knowledge and its application, and between the academe and the outside world' (Moore 2002a,b). Moore and Young have argued that claims for shifting forms of knowledge in the curriculum should not be considered in isolation to 'the role of specialist communities, networks and codes of practice' that are needed to sustain these (Moore and Young 2001: 16). Thus my suggestion of attempting to change curricula towards more integrated forms of knowledge management, such as problem-based learning, will in fact, they believe, have implications for the forms of social organization that underpin curriculum delivery. In particular, it will mean that staff need to reach agreement as to what counts as valid knowledge and how that is to be enacted and recognized within a curriculum. Such discussions do tend to occur when staff seek to transform a whole curriculum from a traditional format to a problem-based one. I would argue that many such curricula meet the criteria suggested by Bernstein for an integrated curriculum, but whether these actually succeed over time is still open to debate.

The dominant challenges of utilizing problem-based learning in the UK seem to centre predominantly on the difficulties of promoting integration of problem-based learning into some kind of framework that spans the modular system in ways that Bernstein suggested. He stipulated four conditions for an integrated-type model to succeed:

1. There must be consensus about the integrating idea and it must be very explicit . . . It may be that integrated codes will only work when there is a high level of ideological consensus among the staff.
2. The nature of the linkage between the integrating idea and the knowledge to be coordinated must be coherently spelled out . . . The development of

Table 10.1 Curriculum models and problem-based learning: a schema

	Fit with problem-based learning	Role of tutor	Student experience	Dominant types of assessment used
Structural design models				
Serviced modular	Poor: tends to create disjunction between discipline	Supplier and integrator of propositional knowledge	Expected to manage interface of PBL and propositional knowledge	Examinations, multiple-choice questions, essays
Notion modular	Can be good, particularly if scenarios occur across modules	Facilitator of learning across subjects and disciplines	Helped to manage knowledge and skills through PBL	Case-based essays, practicals, vivas, portfolios
Genuine modular	Poor across curriculum but tends to be good within discrete modules	Guide to knowledge management	Often experience multiple forms of PBL	Essays, examinations
Process design models				
Content model	Tends to develop model 1 PBL for epistemological competence	Supplier and integrator of propositional knowledge	Receivers of knowledge who acquire propositional knowledge through problem-solving	Examinations, multiple-choice questions, essays
Learning model	Generally poor: PBL seen as just another learning strategy and tends to result in problem-solving learning	Creator of learning conditions to facilitate development of memory and expertise	Learn skills and strategies to manage knowledge and pass course	Multiple-choice questions, practical skills tests, tripartite assessment
Process model	Good but scenarios may be nebulous	Orchestrator of opportunities for learning (in its widest sense)	Learn to manage knowledge but can feel a precarious process	Portfolios, patchwork text, reflective essays

Intentional design models

Constructively aligned model	Good if focus is not on manipulating students or having too much focus on outcomes	Coordinator of knowledge and skill acquisition across boundaries of both	Integrators of knowledge and skills across boundaries. Prevented if strong focus on outcomes	Collaborative assessment essays, case-based essays
Complexity model	Excellent and can be adapted according to discipline	Challenger and decoder of cultures, disciplines and traditions	Supported but encouraged to become independent and critical learners	Patchwork text, case-based, peer- and self-assessed work
Capability model	Good if linked well to content, poor if not	Orchestrator of opportunities for learning (in its widest sense)	Managers of content and capabilities. May be dis-parate or integrated depending on relationship between content and capabilities	Practicals to assess skills, learning contracts, reflective accounts

Abbreviation: PBL = Problem-based learning

such a coordinating framework will be the process of socialisation of the teachers into the code . . .

3. A committee system of staff may have to be set up to create a sensitive feed-back system and which will provide a further agency of socialisation of the code . . .

4. One of the major difficulties inherent in an integrated code arises over what is to be assessed and the form of the assessment . . . Of greatest importance, very clear criteria of evaluation must be worked out . . .

(Bernstein 1975: 84, 107–8)

Many of the difficulties in the UK stem from attempts to fit problem-based learning into constrained existing structures and thus curriculum formation, like many other aspects in higher education, just becomes the managing of control systems. There is a sense that we need to order everything before learning can take place. As we know, a curriculum is not just a list of knowledge and a series of lecture slots but a form of social practice with procedures, values, histories and identities. Perhaps what is needed as a starting point is a position of critical inter-disciplinarity, a position of acknowledging that there are no disciplinary givens (Barnett 2000a : 104). Yet those who attempt such a move will no doubt have to develop some kind of epistemic community that understands the particular conjunction of disciplines. Moore has argued that

Curriculum projects alone (without a formal organisational base) may not be sufficient to hold people in a new epistemic community, particularly when there are competing priorities, and there is the gravity of other formal organizational structures which distribute resources and rewards, and which unambiguously affirm identity and membership.

(Moore 2002b)

If we were to embrace, wholeheartedly, constructivism as an approach to curriculum formation – which would include students being creators of communi-cative spaces and territories for learning, and developed integrating codes within a framework of critical contestability – this may help us to begin to construct curricula for problem-based learning that transcend the difficulties inherent in inward- and outward-looking curricula. Thus in my utopian view of how problem-based learning curricula might be conceived would be the image that rival discourses would be celebrated and contested and argument would form the organ-izing principles of curriculum formation.

Conclusion

The models, schema and frameworks presented here represent much of the new imaging that is occurring within UK higher education about how we can move away from a rational curriculum planning model. Some of the models fit well with problem-based learning, others do not. What is important, however, is that we move away from tightly bounded structures that prevent students from becoming critical beings who know how to manage knowledge and develop the capabilities they feel they require to be equipped for the world of work. Inevitably, the type of problem-based learning used, the curriculum onto which it is placed and the quality of teachers' and students' experience will vary from institution to institution and country to country. What matters is that we are moving away from the regulatory frameworks of the modular years . . . to more imaginative possibilities.

Epilogue: Changing places or changing spaces?

This book has explored facilitation at a number of different levels, facilitation from staff perspectives, the impact of problem-based learning on assessment, educational and curriculum development. It has also examined more recent issues relating to facilitation, such as the emergence of virtual communities and the influence of plagiarism. The growth of problem-based learning means that conceptions of facilitation continue to change but, I would argue, they need to change to a position where facilitation at whatever level is, and continues to be, contested ground.

Changing places or changing spaces?

Facilitation can be seen as just a shift in position, a changing place or it can be seen as something larger, a shift in the way knowledge spaces are used. For example, for some, facilitation is just a shift in pedagogy, a change in place. The consequence is that staff see their role as facilitator as just that, doing something slightly different. For the institution it is just a new and fashionable learning approach that will help to bring some money into the coffers and for students it may be just a shift in knowledge management: the 'fofo method' or 'diy learning'. Some have chosen to implement problem-based learning this way and it has worked after a fashion, and for many who just see it as a bit of a change or something different to do, the change does not last long. Yet it would appear that this is not the case when we look at the impact of problem-based learning on the lives of staff, students and, in some cases, institutions.

Problem-based learning has prompted change, but it has also been used at a point of change in global higher education. It has prompted change because those implementing it have realized that much of what occurs when moving to a problem-based approach to learning and curriculum design is not just a shift in roles, it is about using spaces differently. The result is that notions of space, learning and facilitation have changed. Often things that were not really considered to be learning spaces are now acknowledged as such – for example, common rooms, interactive library spaces, chat rooms and cafes. Learning is seen less and less as the province of the teacher and a new dialogic space has emerged where knowledge is contested and what it means to facilitate learning is now negotiated. Students are using the consumer culture to demand more learning that has personal meaning and staff have realized that facilitation may cost them more personally than traditional approaches, which did not necessarily demand that they engaged themselves in the learning process.

Higher education is changing through massification and consumerization and also through a shifting culture from within. In the UK, the demand for institutions to educate large numbers of students and widen participation is resulting in the size, structure and forms of learning all shifting. The use of new learning communities through online and distance education means that students are not only more diverse because of the push to widen participation, but also because more people have access to online learning resources than previously. There has been a realization, too, that perhaps the shift to make all institutions of higher education in the UK into universities was not necessarily a useful change, and that 'new universities' and 'old universities' should now be valued for what they each do best, rather than always being measured against each other with the same criteria. New universities are hot on the trail of education for the allied health professions, widening participation while at the same time providing excellent teaching and doing some research. The old universities undertake sound research, solid, usually traditional teaching and are having a go at widening participation. More of the same in higher education has not really been a useful strategy and the divide between the old and the new has just meant greater pressure for those at the lower end of the hierarchy. Yet problem-based learning has flourished at this point of change, more in the new sector in the UK than the old.

This is not the case worldwide, where many eminent universities have taken it up. What appears to be happening is that it is being recognized that problem-based learning is an approach to learning, and to life, that can help with the rapid changes in university systems, learning and knowledge spaces. With the emergence of the Internet and new forms of geography, there has been a move away from the idea of things being ordered and linear and a shift towards the idea that we have created spatial zones and imaginary geography. The result is that the boundaries around conceptions of time and space have moved and so we have created different kinds of spaces and we have developed a language that reflects this. For example, things that we once saw as stable boundaries no longer exist, such as boundaries between home and work, printed text and electronic text. Global space means that space and time become almost interchangeable, since one necessarily orders the other, and everything shifts and moves in relation to everything else. Thus learning, knowledge, relationships, communication, home and workplaces are no longer static, bounded and uniform but instead on-going, variable and emergent. The result has not only been the creating of new forms of learning to accommodate this, but also the development of different kinds of online learning communities, which have largely emerged from the types of online education available. Thus problem-based learning is helping with change in higher education, because it is a flexible approach that can be used to meet a number of complex aims, such as increased student numbers, virtual communities and the need to manage the knowledge explosion – from both a staff and student perspective.

Uncertain endings

So, what of my arguments about perspectives on facilitation in higher education? Facilitation does need to be construed more broadly than just helping students to learn in small groups. Barnett has suggested that:

> Higher education, then, faces up to the challenging of frameworks that characterizes supercomplexity by enabling students to sense that the frameworks through which we seek to understand the world are themselves challengeable. To repeat, this handling of uncertainty is a matter of living effectively not so much with cognitive uncertainty but with experiential uncertainty.

(Barnett 2000a: 154)

Although I would argue that it is not really possible to distinguish between cognitive and experiential uncertainty, since they would seem to be inextricably linked in higher education, the point that Barnett is making is that managing uncertainty is part of learning and knowledge management. To embrace such uncertainty, problem-based learning curricula need to be deconstructed. Reconstruction will involve a clear view of what curriculum-making really involves, while acknowledging the importance of the existence of new learning spaces and places for knowledge creation, along with methods of assessment that match. Facilitation is not about a change in places, it is about a radical repositioning of the curriculum and, with that, learners and teachers. To leave facilitation in problem-based learning as something narrowly construed that will help to develop key skills, equip students for the world of work and meet the most recent political agendas is to leave it behind in modernity. What is required is a repositioning of facilitation and problem-based learning in a different space. A space where it is recognized that fragmentation, reflexivity, new spatial zones and a shifting landscape of knowledge will be a large component of the geography of higher education in the future. Facilitating problem-based learning demands that we embrace such change.

Glossary

Collaborative assessment: where the student assesses herself or himself in light of the criteria agreed with the tutor. The tutor assesses the student using the same criteria and they negotiate a final grade.

Critical contestability: a position whereby students understand and acknowledge the transient nature of subject and discipline boundaries. They are able to transcend and inter-rogate these boundaries through a commitment to exploring the subtext of subjects and disciplines.

Dialogic learning: learning that occurs when insights and understandings emerge through dialogue in a learning environment. It is a form of learning in which students draw upon their own experience to explain the concepts and ideas with which they are presented, and then use that experience to make sense for themselves and also to explore further issues.

Domain: the overlapping spheres within each stance. The borders of the domains merge with one another and, therefore, shifts between domains are transitional areas where particu-lar kinds of learning occur.

Feedback session: a session in which students feed back to the problem-based learning team the information they have discovered which relates to the problem scenario.

Frame factors: issues that are raised by the students that do not relate directly to the problem scenario. For example, transport between campuses, the arrival of student uniforms or students' personal problems.

Interactional stance: the ways in which learners work and learn in groups and construct meaning in relation to one another.

Inter-peer assessment: when students from a problem-based learning team assess the work of another team.

Inter-professional education: the use of a variety of teaching methods and learning strategies to encourage interaction and interactive learning across the professions, which includes the development of skills and attitudes as well as knowledge.

Intra-peer assessment: students assess the product of what they themselves have produced as a team.

Introductory session: the first problem-based learning session in which the problem scenario is presented to the students.

Key skills: skills such as working with others, problem-solving and improving personal learning and performance, which students are expected to require for the world of work.

Learner identity: an identity formulated through the interaction of learner and learning. The notion of learner identity moves beyond, but encapsulates, the notion of learning style and encompasses positions that students take up in learning situations, whether consciously or unconsciously.

Learning context: the interplay of all the values, beliefs, relationships, frameworks and external structures that operate within a given learning environment.

Learning in relation: the ways in which students learn with and through others to help them to make connections between their lives, with other subjects and disciplines and with personal concerns. Learning in relation also incorporates not only the idea that students learn in relation to their own knowledge and experience, but also to that of others.

Learner stances: the three stances (personal, pedagogical and interactions) that together form the framework of Dimensions of Learner Experience.

Mode 1 Knowledge (Gibbons *et al.* 1994): propositional knowledge that is produced within academe separate from its use. The academe is considered the traditional environment for the generation of mode 1 knowledge.

Mode 2 Knowledge (Gibbons *et al.* 1994): knowledge that transcends disciplines and is produced in, and validated through, the world of work. Knowing in this mode demands the integration of skills and abilities to act in a particular context.

Pedagogical stance: the ways in which people see themselves as learners in particular educational environments.

Peer assessment: involves students making judgements about other students' work. Ideally, the students design their own assessment criteria and use them to assess each other, but in many programmes they are designed by staff.

Performative slide: the increasing focus in higher education on what students are able to *do*, which has emerged from the desire to equip students for life and work. Higher education is sliding towards encouraging students to perform rather than to critique and do.

Personal stance: the way in which staff and students see themselves in relation to the learning context and give their own distinctive meaning to their experience of that context.

Problem-based learning team: several students (8–10) who work together as a defined group.

Problem-solving learning: teaching in which the focus is on students solving a given problem by acquiring the answers expected by the lecturer, answers that are rooted in the information supplied in some way to the students. The solutions are bounded by the content and students are expected to explore little extra material, other than that with which they have been provided, to discover the solutions.

Self-assessment: this involves students developing standards to apply to their work and making judgements about the extent to which they have met these criteria.

Shared learning: any learning or teaching in which participants are drawn from two or more professional or disciplinary groups, which may include workshops and seminars as well as lectures.

Stance: one's attitude, belief or disposition towards a particular context, person or experience. It refers to a particular position one takes up in life towards something, at a particular point in time.

Team: a group of people who work together with a common purpose. There is a limited membership and the team has the power to make decisions. Teams have a focus, a set of team rules and are time-limited.

Transition: shifts in learner experience caused by a challenge to the person's life-world. Transitions occur in particular areas of students' lives, at different times and in distinct ways. The notion of transition carries with it the idea of movement from one place to another and with it the necessity of taking up a new position in a different place.

Transitional learning: learning that occurs as a result of critical reflection upon shifts (transitions) that have taken place for the students personally (including viscerally), pedagogically and/or interactionally.

Bibliography

Almy, T.P., Colby, K.K., Zubkoff, M., Gephart, D.S., Moore-West, M. and Lundquist, L.L. (1992) Health, society, and the physician: problem-based learning of the social sciences and humanities, *Annals of Internal Medicine*, 116(7): 569–74.

Atkinson, T. (2000) Learning to teach: intuitive skills and reasoned objectivity, in T. Atkinson and G. Claxton (eds) *The Intuitive Practitioner*. Buckingham: SRHE/Open University Press.

Bales, R. (1950) *Interaction Process Analysis*. Cambridge, MA: Addison-Wesley.

Bales, R. (1970) *Personality and Interpersonal Behaviour*. New York: Holt, Rinehart & Winston.

Barnett, R. (1994) *The Limits of Competence*. Buckingham: SRHE/Open University Press.

Barnett, R. (1997) *Higher Education: A Critical Business*. Buckingham: SRHE/Open University Press.

Barnett, R. (2000a) *Realizing the University in an Age of Supercomplexity*. Buckingham: SRHE/Open University Press.

Barnett, R. (2000b) Supercomplexity and the curriculum, *Studies in High Education*, 25(3): 254–65.

Barnett, R. and Coates, K. (2002) Conceptualizing curricula: a schema. *Imaginative Curriculum Knowledge Development Paper* 2 April. LTSN Generic Centre, www.ltsn.ac.uk/genericcentre (accessed 20 May 2002).

Barrett, T. (2001) Philosophical principles for problem-based learning: Freire's concepts of personal development and social empowerment, in *Proceedings of the 3rd Asia Pacific Conference on Problem-based Learning*, Rockhampton, 9–12 December.

Barrows, H.S. and Tamblyn, R.M. (1980) *Problem-based Learning: An Approach to Medical Education*. New York: Springer.

Belbin, R.M. (1993) *Team Roles at Work*. Oxford: Buttterworth-Heinemann.

Belenky, M.F., Clinchy, B.M., Goldberger, N.R. and Tarule, J.M. (1986) *Women's Ways of Knowing*. New York: Basic Books.

Bernstein, B. (1971) On the classification and framing of educational knowledge, in M.F.D. Young (ed.) *Knowledge and Control*. London: Collier-Macmillan.

Bernstein, B. (1975) *On the Classification and Framing of Educational Knowledge: Class, Codes and Control. Vol. 3: Towards a Theory of Educational Transmissions*. London: Routledge & Kegan Paul.

Bernstein, B. (1996) *Pedagogy, Symbolic Control and Identity*. London: Taylor & Francis.

Biggs, J. (1999) *Teaching for Quality Learning at University*. Buckingham: SRHE/Open University Press.

Biggs, J. (2002) Conceptualizing the curriculum through the idea of constructive alignment. *Imaginative Curriculum Knowledge Development Paper* 2 April. LTSN Generic Centre, www.ltsn.ac.uk/genericcentre (accessed 20 May 2002).

Bligh, J., Lloyd-Jones, G. and Smith, G. (2000) Early effects of new problem-based clinically oriented curriculum on students' perceptions of teaching, *Medical Education*, 36(6): 487–9.

Bloom, B.S. (ed.) (1956) *Taxonomy of Educational Objectives: The Classification of Educational Goals*. New York: Longman.

Bormann, E. (1972) Fantasy and rhetorical vision: the rhetorical criticism of social reality, *Quarterly Journal of Speech*, 58: 396–407.

Boud, D. (ed.) (1985) *Problem-based Learning in Education for the Professions*. Sydney, NSW: Higher Education Research and Development Society of Australasia.

Boud, D. (1986) *Implementing Student Self-Assessment*. HERDSA Green Guide No. 5. Sydney, NSW: Higher Education Research and Development Society of Australasia.

Boud, D. (1990) Assessment and the promotion of academic values, *Studies in Higher Education*, 15(1): 101–11.

Boud, D. (2000) Sustainable assessment: rethinking assessment for the learning society, *Studies in Continuing Education*, 22(2): 151–67.

Boud, D. and Feletti, G. (eds) (1997) *The Challenge of Problem Based Learning*, 2nd edn. London: Kogan Page.

Boud, D. and Miller, N. (eds) (1996) *Working with Experience: Animating Learning*. London: Kogan Page.

Bourdieu, P. (1975) The specificity of the scientific field and the social conditions of progress of reason, *Social Science Information*, 14(6): 299–316.

Britain, S. and Liber, O. (2000) *A Framework for Pedagogical Evaluation of Virtual Learning Environments*, http://www.jisc.ac.uk/jtap/htm/jtap-o41.html (accessed on 21 September 2002).

Brookfield, S.D. (1985) *Becoming a Critically Reflective Teacher*. San Francisco, CA: Jossey-Bass.

Carroll, J. (2002) *A Handbook for Deterring Plagiarism in Higher Education*. Oxford: Oxford Centre for Staff and Learning Development.

Chester, G. (2001) *Plagiarism Detection and Prevention: Final Report on the JISC Electronic Detection Project*, http://www.jisc.ac.uk/mle/plagiarism (accessed on 7 September 2002).

Clark, B. (1980) *Academic Culture*, Working Paper No. 42. New Haven, CN: Yale University Higher Education Research Group.

Claxton, G. (2000) The anatomy of intuition, in T. Atkinson and G. Claxton (eds) *The Intuitive Practitioner*. Buckingham: SRHE/Open University Press.

Coffield, F. and Williamson, B. (eds) (1997) *Repositioning Higher Education*. Buckingham: SRHE/Open University Press.

Committee of Scottish University Principles (1992) *Teaching and Learning in an Expanding Higher Education System* (convened by Professor A.G. MacFarlane). Edinburgh: SCFC.

Cormack, D. (1989) *Team Spirit*. Michigan: Zondervan.

Crawley, R.M. (1999) *Evaluating CSCL – Theorists' and Users' Perspectives*, http://www.bton.ac.uk/cscl/jtap/paper1.htm (accessed 8 November 2001).

Custer, R.L. (1994) *Performance-Based Education Implementation Handbook*. Columbia, MO: Instructional Materials Lab, University of Missouri.

Day, C. and Hadfield, M. (1996) Metaphors for movement: accounts of professional development, in M. Kompf, W. Bond, D. Dworet and R. Boak (eds) *Changing Research and Practice: Teachers' Professionalism, Identities and Knowledge*. London: Falmer Press.

Day, R. and Williams, B. (2000) Development of critical thinking through problem-based learning: a pilot study, *Journal on Excellence in College Teaching*, 11(2/3): 203–26.

Deem, R. (1998) New managerialism and higher education: the management of performances and cultures in universities in the United Kingdom, *International Studies in
Sociology of Education*, 8(1): 47–70.

De Grave, W.S., Dolmans, D.H.J.M. and van der Vleuten, C.P.M. (1998) Tutor intervention
profile: reliability and validity, *Medical Education*, 32(3): 262–8.

De Grave, W.S., Dolmans, D.H.J.M. and van der Vleuten, C.P.M. (1999) Profiles of effective
tutors in problem-based learning: scaffolding students' learning, *Medical Education*,
33(12): 901–6.

Del Mar, C.B. (1997) Training GPs in problem-based learning, in J. Conway, R. Fisher,
L. Sheridan-Burns and G. Ryan (eds) *Research and Development in Problem Based Learning:
Integrity, Innovation, Integration*, 4: 110–13.

Denzin, N. (1989) *Interpretive Interactionism*. London: Sage.

Denzin, N. and Lincoln, Y. (1994) *Handbook of Qualitative Research*. London: Sage.

Dewey, J. (1938) *Experience and Education*. New York: Collier and Kappa Delta Phi.

Dolmans, D.H.J.M., Wolfhagen, I.H.A.P. and Snellen-Balendong, H.A.M. (1994a)
Improving the effectiveness of tutors in problem-based learning, *Medical Teacher*, 16(4):
369–77.

Dolmans, D.H.J.M., Wolfhagen, I.H.A.P., Schmidt, H.G. and Van der Vleuten, C.P.M.
(1994b) A rating scale for tutor evaluation in a problem-based curriculum: validity and
reliability, *Medical Education*, 28(6): 550–8.

Donnelly, R. (2002) *Online Learning in Teacher Education: Enhanced with a Problem-based Learning
Approach*. Mimeo, Dublin Institute of Technology, Dublin, Ireland.

Duch, B.J., Groh, S.E. and Allen, D.E. (2001) *The Power of Problem-based Learning*. Sterling,
VA: Stylus Publishing.

Eden, C. and Radford, J. (1990) *Tackling Strategic Problems: The Role of Group Decision Support*.
London: Sage.

Edwards, R. (1997) *Changing Places*. London: Routledge.

Eliot, G. (1872) *Middlemarch*. London: Penguin.

Eraut, M. (2000) The intuitive practitioner: a critical overview, in T. Atkinson and
G. Claxton (eds) *The Intuitive Practitioner*. Buckingham: SHRE/Open University Press.

Foss, S. (1989) *Rhetorical Criticism*. Prospect Heights, IL: Waveland Press.

Foucault, M. (1979) *Discipline and Punish: The Birth of the Prison*. Harmondsworth: Penguin.

Franklyn-Stokes, A. and Newstead, S.E. (1995) Undergraduate cheating: who does what and
why, *Studies in High Education*, 20(2): 159–72.

Freire, P. (1972) *Pedagogy of the Oppressed*. London: Penguin.

Garrison, D.R. (1993) A cognitive constructivist view of distance education: an analysis of
teaching-learning assumptions, *Distance Education*, 14(2): 199–211.

Gibbons, M., Limoges, C., Nowotny, H., Schwarzman, S., Scott, P. and Trow, M. (1994) *The
New Production of Knowledge: The Dynamics of Science and Research in Contemporary Societies*.
London: Sage.

Gibbs, G. (1992) Improving the quality of student learning through course design, in
R. Barnett (ed.) *Learning to Effect*. Milton Keynes: SRHE/Open University Press.

Gibbs, G., Habeshaw, T. and Yorke, M. (2000) The use of institutional learning and teaching
strategies in English higher education, *Higher Education*, 40: 351–72.

Gijselaers, W.H. (1997) Effects of contextual factors on tutor behaviour, *Teaching and Learning
in Medicine*, 9(2): 116–24.

Gijselaers, W.H. and Schmidt, H.G. (1990) Development and evaluation of a causal model
of problem-based learning, in A.M. Nooman, H.G. Schmidt and E. Ezzat (eds) *Innovation in Medical Education: An Evaluation of its Present Status*. New York: Springer.

Glen, S. and Wilkie, K. (2000) *Problem-based Learning in Nursing*. London: Macmillan.

Goodlad, S. (1995) *The Quest for Quality: Sixteen Forms of Heresy in Higher Education*. Buckingham: SHRE/Open University Press.

Greenley, S. (2002) *Problem-based Learning and Nursing Libraries: The UK Experience*, UK PBL website, http://www.hss.coventry.ac.uk/pbl/Documents/PBL Report-UKPBL website .doc (accessed 17 September 2002).

Habermas, J. (1989) *The Theory of Communicative Action*, Vol. 2. Cambridge: Polity Press.

Haggis, T. (2002) Exploring the 'black box' of process: a comparison of theoretical notions of the 'adult learner' with accounts of postgraduate learning experience, *Studies in Higher Education*, 27(2): 207–20.

Hammel, J., Royeen, C.B., Bagatell, N., Chandler, B., Jensen, G., Loveland, J. and Stone, G. (1999) Students' perspectives on problem-based learning in an occupational therapy curriculum: a multiyear qualitative evaluation, *American Journal of Occupational Therapy*, 53(2): 199–206.

Hannan, A. and Silver, H. (2000) *Innovating in Higher Education: Teaching, Learning and Institutional Cultures*. Buckingham: SRHE/Open University Press.

Hannan, A., English, S. and Silver, H. (1999) Why innovate?, *Studies in Higher Education*, 24(3): 279–89.

Harris, R. (2001) *The Plagiarism Handbook*. Los Angeles, CA: Pyrczak Publishing.

Henkel, M. (2000) *Academic Identities and Policy Change in Higher Education*. London: Jessica Kingsley.

Henri, F. and Rigault, C. (1996) Collaborative distance education and computer conferencing, in T. Liao (ed.) *Advanced Educational Technology: Research Issues and Future Potential*. Berlin: Springer.

Heron, J. (1988) Assessment revisited, in D. Boud (ed.) *Developing Student Autonomy in Learning*. London: Kogan Page.

Heron, J. (1989) *The Facilitator's Handbook*. London: Kogan Page.

Heron, J. (1993) *Group Facilitation*. London: Kogan Page.

Holmes, D.B. and Kaufman, D.M. (1994) Tutoring in problem-based learning: a teacher development process, *Medical Education*, 28(4): 275–83.

Jackson, N. and Shaw, M. (2002) Conceptions and visual representations of the curriculum. *Imaginative Curriculum Knowledge Development Paper* 2 April, LTSN Generic Centre, www.ltsn.ac.uk/genericcentre (accessed 20 May 2002).

Jacobsen, D.Y. (1997) Tutorial processes in a problem-based learning context: medical students reception and negotiations. Unpublished doctoral dissertation, Norwegian University of Science and Technology, Norway.

Jaques, D. (2000) *Learning in Groups*. London: Croom Helm.

Jarvis, P. (1987) *Adult Learning in the Social Context*. London: Croom Helm.

Kandlbinder, P. and Maufette, Y. (2001) Perceptions of teaching by science teachers using a student-centred approach, in *Proceedings of the 3rd Asia Pacific Conference on Problem-based Learning*, Rockhampton, 9–12 December.

Kaufman, D.M. and Holmes, D.B. (1998) The relationship of tutors' content expertise to interventions and perceptions in a problem-based learning medical curriculum, *Medical Education*, 32(3): 255–61.

Kaye, A.R. (1992) Learning together apart, in A.R. Kaye (ed.) *Collaborative Learning through Computer Conferencing*. London: Springer.

King, S (2001) Problem-based induction program for first year students, communication to the *3rd Asia Pacific Conference on Problem-based Learning*, Rockhampton, 9–12 December.

Kippers, V., Price, D. and Isaacs, G. (1997) An evaluation of problem-based learning (PBL) facilitator training program, in J. Conway, R. Fisher, L. Sheridan-Burns and

G. Ryan (eds) *Research and Development in Problem Based Learning: Integrity, Innovation, Integration*, 4: 262–74.

Kliebard, H.M. (1968) Curricular objectives and evaluation: a reassessment, *The High School Journal*, 3: 241–7.

Knight, P. (1995) *Assessment for Learning in Higher Education*. London: Kogan Page.

Knight, P. (2001) *A Briefing on Key Concepts: Formative and Summative, Criterion and Norm-referenced Assessment*. LTSN Generic Centre Assessment Series No.7. York: LTSN Generic Centre.

Knight, P. (2002) A process approach to curriculum making to support complex learning. *Imaginative Curriculum Knowledge Development Paper* 2 April, LTSN Generic Centre, www.ltsn.ac.uk/genericcentre (accessed 20 May 2002).

Lahteenmaki, M. (2001) Problem-based learning during the first academic year, in *Proceedings of the 3rd Asia Pacific Conference on Problem-based Learning*, Rockhampton, 9–12 December.

Laurillard, D. (1993) *Rethinking University Teaching: A Framework for the Effective Use of Educational Technology*. London: Routledge.

Liddle, M. (2000) Student attitudes toward problem-based learning in law, *Journal on Excellence in College Teaching*, 11(2/3): 163–90.

Lincoln, Y. and Guba, E. (1985) *Naturalistic Inquiry*. London: Sage.

Little, S. (1997) Preparing tertiary teachers for problem-based learning, in D. Boud and G. Feletti (eds) *The Challenge of Problem Based Learning*, 2nd edn. London: Kogan Page.

Macdonald, R. and Savin-Baden, M. (2003) *A Briefing on Assessment in Problem-Based Learning*. LTSN Generic Centre Assessment Series No.7. York: LTSN Generic Centre.

MacKinnon, M.M. (1999) PBL in Hong Kong: three approaches to curriculum reform, *PBL Insight*, 2(2): 1–6, http://www.samford.edu/pbl/ (accessed 20 August 2002).

Majoor, J. (1999) The challenges of problem-based teaching: a reply to Maudsley, G., *British Medical Journal*, 318: 657–61.

Major, C. (2000) Assessing problem-based learning. *Journal on Excellence in College Teaching*, 11(2/3): 113–31.

Margetson, D. (1993) Education, pedagogy and problem-based learning, in A.R. Viskovic (ed.) *Research and Development in Higher Education*, Vol. 14. Sydney, NSW: Higher Education Research and Development Society of Australasia.

Marton, F. and Säljö, R. (1984) Approaches to learning, in F. Marton, D. Hounsell and N.J. Entwistle (eds) *The Experience of Learning*. Edinburgh: Scottish Academic Press.

Mason, R. (1998) Models of online courses, *ALN Magazine* 2(2), http://www..aln.org/alnweb/magazine/vol2_issue2/Masonfinal.htm (accessed on 20 September 1999).

McGill, I. and Beaty, L. (2001) *Action Learning*, 2nd revised edn. London: Kogan Page.

McKenna, C. (2002) An exploration of students' experiences in endomorphic and ecto-morphic modules. Unpublished master's dissertation, Coventry University.

Middlehurst, R. (1995) Changing leadership in universities, in T. Schuller (ed.) *The Changing University?* Buckingham: SRHE/Open University Press.

Miller, C.M.L. and Parlett, M. (1974) *Up to the Mark: A Study of the Examination Game*. London: Society for Research into Higher Education.

Moore, R. (2002a) Policy-driven curriculum restructuring: academic identities in transition?, Communication to the *Higher Education Close Up Conference 2*, University of Lancaster, 16–18 July.

Moore, R. (2002b) Between covenant and contract: negotiating academic pedagogic identities, communication to *Kenton Education Association Conference*, Muldersdrift, South Africa, November.

Moore, R. and Young, M. (2001) Knowledge and the curriculum in the sociology of education: towards a reconceptualisation, *British Journal of Sociology of Education*, 22(4): 445–61.

Mpofu, D.J.S., Das, M., Stewart, T., Dunn, E. and Schmidt, H. (1998) Perceptions of group dynamics in problem-based learning session: a time to reflect on group issues, *Medical Teacher*, (20)5: 421–7.

Murray, I. and Savin-Baden, M. (2000) Staff development in problem-based learning, *Teaching in Higher Education*, 5(1): 107–26.

National Committee of Inquiry into Higher Education (1997) *Higher Education in the Learning Society* (Report of the National Committee of Inquiry into Higher Education chaired by Sir Ron Dearing). London: HMSO.

Nayer, M. (1995) Faculty development for problem-based learning programs, *Teaching and Learning in Medicine*, 7(3): 138–48.

Neame, R.L.B. (1982) Academic roles and satisfaction in a problem-based medical curriculum, *Studies in Higher Education*, 7(2): 141–51.

Neville, A.J. (1999) The problem-based learning tutor: teacher? facilitator? evaluator?, *Medical Teacher*, 21(4): 393–401.

Niemi, H. and Kemmis, S. (1999) Communicative evaluation, *Lifelong Learning in Europe*, 4(1): 55–64.

Norman, G. (1997) Assessment in problem-based learning, in D. Boud and G. Feletti (eds) *The Challenge of Problem Based Learning*, 2nd edn. London: Kogan Page.

Painvin, C., Neufeld, V., Norman, G., Walker, I. and Whelan, G. (1979) The 'triple jump' exercise: a structured measure of problem-solving and self-directed learning, in *Proceedings of the 18th Annual Conference on Research in Medical Education*, Washington DC, November.

Pau, A.K., Collinson, S. and Croucher, R. (1999) Dental students' evaluation of 2 community-oriented PBL, *European Journal of Dental Education*, 3(4): 159–66.

Pearson, M. and Smith, D. (1985) Debriefing in experience-based learning, in D. Boud, R. Keogh and D. Walker (eds) *Reflection: Turning Experience into Learning*. London: Kogan Page.

Perry, W.G. (1970) *Forms of Intellectual and Ethical Development During the College Years: A Scheme.* New York: Holt, Rinehart & Winston.

Perry, W.G. (1988) Different worlds in the same classroom, in P. Ramsden (ed.) *Improving Learning: New Perspectives*. London: Kogan Page.

Peters, R.S. (1959) *Authority, Responsibility and Education*. London: Allen & Unwin.

Phillips, L.D. and Phillips, M.C. (1993) Facilitated work groups: theory and practice, *Journal of Operational Research Society*, 44(6): 533–49.

Powles, A., Wintrip, N., Neufeld, V., Wakefield, J., Coates, G. and Burrows, J. (1981) The 'triple jump' exercise: further studies of an evaluative technique, in *Proceedings of the 20th Annual Conference on Research in Medical Education*, Washington DC, November.

Pritchard, C. (2000) *Making Managers in Universities and Colleges*. Buckingham: SRHE/Open University Press.

Quinlan, K. (2000) An evaluation of a literature database to support problem-based learning, *Journal on Excellence in College Teaching*, 11(2/3): 27–39.

Rappaport, J. (1981) In praise of paradox: a social policy of empowerment over prevention, *American Journal of Community Psychology*, (9): 1–25.

Reason, P. and Rowan, J. (eds) (1981) *Human Inquiry – A Sourcebook of New Paradigm Research*. New York: Wiley.

Regehr, G. and Norman, G. (1996) Issues in cognitive psychology: implications for professional education, *Academic Medicine*, 71(9): 988–1001.

Rendas, A., Pinto, P.R. and Gambosa, T. (1999) A computer simulation designed for problem-based learning, *Medical Education*, 93: 47–54.

Rogers, C. (1983) *Freedom to Learn for the '80's*. Columbus, OH: Merrill.

Ryan, G. (1993) Student perceptions about self-directed learning in a professional course implementing problem-based learning, *Studies in Higher Education*, 18(1): 53–63.

Ryan, G. (1997) Promoting educational integrity in PBL programs – choosing carefully and implementing wisely, in J. Conway, R. Fisher, L. Sheridan-Burns and G. Ryan (eds) *Research and Development in Problem Based Learning: Integrity, Innovation, Integration*, 4: 546–59.

Salmon, G. (2000) *E-Moderating: The Key to Teaching and Learning Online*. London: Kogan Page.

Savin, M. (1987) Problem-based learning from the learner's perspective. Unpublished master's dissertation, University of London, Institute of Education.

Savin-Baden, M. (1996) Problem-based learning: a catalyst for enabling and disabling disjunction prompting transitions in learner stances? Unpublished doctoral dissertation, University of London, Institute of Education.

Savin-Baden, M. (2000a) *Problem-based Learning in Higher Education: Untold Stories*. Buckingham: SRHE/Open University Press.

Savin-Baden, M. (2000b) Facilitating problem-based learning: the impact of tutors' pedagogical stances, *Journal on Excellence in College Teaching*, 11(2/3): 97–111.

Savin-Baden, M. (2002) Deconstructing problem-based learning facilitation, Keynote speech to *PBL 2002: A Pathway to Better Learning*, Baltimore, MD, 16–20 June.

Savin-Baden, M. and Fisher, A. (2002) Negotiating honesties in the research process, *British Journal of Occupational Therapy*, 65(4): 191–3.

Savin-Baden, M. and Wilkie, K. (2001) Understanding and utilising problem-based learning strategically in higher education, in C. Rust (ed.) *Improving Student Learning Strategically*, Proceedings of 8th Improving Students Learning Symposium. Oxford: The Oxford Centre for Tutor and Learning Development.

Scardemalia, M. and Bereiter, C. (1994) Computer support for knowledge-building communities, *The Journal of the Learning Sciences*, 3(3): 256–83.

Schmidt, H. and Moust, J. (2000) Towards a taxonomy of problems used in problem-based learning curricula, *Journal on Excellence in College Teaching*, 11(2/3): 57–72.

Scott, P. (1995) *The Meanings of Mass Higher Education*. Buckingham: SRHE/Open University Press.

Scott, P. (1998) Massification, internationalization and globalization, in P. Scott (ed.) *The Globalization of Higher Education*. Buckingham: SRHE/Open University Press.

Silen, C. (2001) Between chaos and cosmos – a driving force for responsibility and independence in learning, in *Proceedings of the 3rd Asia Pacific Conference on Problem-based Learning*, Rockhampton, 9–12 December.

Stenhouse, L. (1975) *An Introduction to Curriculum Research and Development*. London: Heinemann.

Stephenson, J. (2002) The capability envelope: a framework for a negotiated curriculum, *Imaginative Curriculum Knowledge Development Paper* 2 April, LTSN Generic Centre, www.ltsn.ac.uk/genericcentre (accessed 20 May 2002).

Stronach, I., Corbin, B., McNamara, O., Stark, S. and Warne, T. (2002) Towards an uncertain politics of professionalism: teacher and nurse identities in flux, *Journal of Educational Policy*, 17(1): 109–38.

Taylor, I. (1997) *Developing Learning in Professional Education*. Buckingham: SRHE/Open University Press.

Taylor, I. and Burgess, H. (1995) Orientation to self-directed learning: paradox or paradigm, *Studies in Higher Education*, 20 (1): 87–97.

Trowler, P. (1998) *Academics Responding to Change: New Higher Education Frameworks and Academic Cultures*. Buckingham: SRHE/Open University Press.

Turner, B. (1993) Talcott Parsons, universalism and educational revolution: democracy versus professionalism, *British Journal of Sociology*, 44(1): 1–24.

Usher, R. and Edwards, R. (1994) *Postmodernism and Education*. London: Routledge.

Warburton, B. and Whitehouse, C. (1998) Students' perceptions of a learner-centred approach using problem-based learning on an undergraduate general practice course at the University of Manchester, *Medical Teacher*, 20(6): 590–91.

Wee, K.N.L. and Kek, Y.C. (2002) *Authentic Problem-based learning*. Singapore: Prentice-Hall.

Wegner, S.B. Holloway, K.C. and Wegner, S.K. (1999) The effects of a computer-based instructional management system on students' communication in a distance learning environment, *Educational Technology and Society*, 2(4): 145–53.

Weil, S. and McGill, I. (eds) (1989) *Making Sense of Experiential Learning: Diversity in Theory and Practice*. Buckingham: SRHE/Open University Press.

Wilkerson, L. and Hundert, E.M. (1997) Becoming a problem-based tutor: increasing self-awareness through faculty development, in D. Boud and G. Feletti (eds) *The Challenge of Problem Based Learning*, 2nd edn. London: Kogan Page.

Wilkie, K. (2002) Action, attitudes and attributes: developing facilitation skills for problem-based learning. Unpublished doctoral dissertation, Coventry University.

Winter, R., Buck, A. and Sobiechowska, P. (1999) *Professional Experience and the Investigative Imagination*. London: Routledge.

Index

The Society for Research into Higher Education

The Society for Research into Higher Education (SRHE), an international body, exists to stimulate and coordinate research into all aspects of higher education. It aims to improve the quality of higher education through the encouragement of debate and publication on issues of policy, on the organization and management of higher education institutions, and on the curriculum, teaching and learning methods.

The Society is entirely independent and receives no subsidies, although individual events often receive sponsorship from business or industry. The Society is financed through corporate and individual subscriptions and has members from many parts of the world. It is an NGO of UNESCO.

Under the imprint *SRHE & Open University Press*, the Society is a specialist publisher of research, having over 80 titles in print. In addition to *SRHE News*, the Society's newsletter, the Society publishes three journals: *Studies in Higher Education* (three issues a year), *Higher Education Quarterly* and *Research into Higher Education Abstracts* (three issues a year).

The Society runs frequent conferences, consultations, seminars and other events. The annual conference in December is organized at and with a higher education institution. There are a growing number of networks which focus on particular areas of interest, including:

Access	Learning Environment
Assessment	Legal Education
Consultants	Managing Innovation
Curriculum Development	New Technology for Learning
Eastern European	Postgraduate Issues
Educational Development Research	Quantitative Studies
FE/HE	Student Development
Funding	Vocational Qualifications
Graduate Employment	

Benefits to members

Individual

- The opportunity to participate in the Society's networks
- Reduced rates for the annual conferences
- Free copies of *Research into Higher Education Abstracts*

- Reduced rates for *Studies in Higher Education*
- Reduced rates for *Higher Education Quarterly*
- Free copy of *Register of Members' Research Interests* – includes valuable reference material on research being pursued by the Society's members
- Free copy of occasional in-house publications, e.g. *The Thirtieth Anniversary Seminars Presented by the Vice-Presidents*
- Free copies of *SRHE News* which informs members of the Society's activities and provides a calendar of events, with additional material provided in regular mailings
- A 35 per cent discount on all SRHE/Open University Press books
- The opportunity for you to apply for the annual research grants
- Inclusion of your research in the *Register of Members' Research Interests*

Corporate

- Reduced rates for the annual conference
- The opportunity for members of the Institution to attend SRHE's network events at reduced rates
- Free copies of *Research into Higher Education Abstracts*
- Free copies of *Studies in Higher Education*
- Free copies of *Register of Members' Research Interests* – includes valuable reference material on research being pursued by the Society's members
- Free copy of occasional in-house publications
- Free copies of *SRHE News*
- A 35 per cent discount on all SRHE/Open University Press books
- The opportunity for members of the Institution to submit applications for the Society's research grants
- The opportunity to work with the Society and co-host conferences
- The opportunity to include in the *Register of Members' Research Interests* your Institution's research into aspects of higher education

Membership details: SRHE, 76 Portland Place, London W1B 1NT, UK Tel: 020 7637 2766. Fax: 020 7637 2781. email: srhe@mailbox.ulcc.ac.uk world wide web: http://www.srhe.ac.uk./srhe/ *Catalogue*: SRHE & Open University Press, Celtic Court, 22 Ballmoor, Buckingham MK18 1XW. Tel: 01280 823388. Fax: 01280 823233. email: enquiries@openup.co.uk

BEING A TEACHER IN HIGHER EDUCATION

Peter T. Knight

Being a Teacher in Higher Education draws extensively on research literatures to give detailed advice about the core business of teaching: instruction, learning activities, assessment, planning and getting good evaluations. It offers hundreds of practical suggestions in a collegial rather than didactic style.

This is not, however, another book of tips or heroic success stories. For one thing Peter Knight appreciates the different circumstances that new, part-time and established teachers are in. For another, he insists that teaching well (and enjoying it) is as much about how teachers feel about themselves as it is about how many slick teaching techniques they can string together. He argues that it is important to develop a sense of oneself as a good teacher (particularly in increasingly difficult working conditions); and it is for this reason that the final part of this work is about career management and handling change.

This is a book about doing teaching and being a teacher: about reducing the likelihood of burn-out and improving the chances of getting the psychic rewards that make teaching fulfilling. It is an optimistic book for teachers in universities, many of whom feel that opportunities for professional fulfilment are becoming frozen.

Contents

Part 1 People, times and places – Being at work in higher education – Learning teachers, learning students – Being a new teacher – Feeling motivated – Maintaining teaching vitality – Part-time teaching – Part 2 Teaching practices – Instruction – Learning tasks – Creating feedback – Designing for learning – Getting good evaluations – Part 3 Times of change – Change, experiencing change and making change happen – Managing your career – Being a teacher in higher education – References – Index – The Society for Research into Higher Education.

256pp   0 335 20930 0 (Paperback)   0 335 20931 9 (Hardback)

TEACHING FOR QUALITY LEARNING AT UNIVERSITY
SECOND EDITION

John Biggs

> . . . full of downright good advice for every academic who wants to do something practical to improve his or her students' learning . . . there are very few writers on the subject of university teaching who can engage a reader so personally, express things so clearly, relate research findings so eloquently to personal experience.
>
> Paul Ramsden

Since the first edition of *Teaching for Quality Learning at University*, the tertiary sector has changed dramatically. Individual teachers, as reflective practitioners, still need to make their own decisions about how they are going to get students actively involved in large classes, to teach international students, and to assess in ways that enhance the quality of learning. But now that quality assurance and quality enhancement are required at the institutional level, the concept of constructive alignment is applied to 'the reflective institution', where it becomes a powerful underpinning to quality enhancement procedures.

Also since the first edition, educational technology has become more widespread than expected, leaving some teachers apprehensive about what it might mean for them. A new chapter elaborates on how ET can be used to enhance learning, but with a warning that any tool, electronic or otherwise, is as good as the thoughtful use to which it is put.

This is an accessible, jargon-free guide to all university teachers interested in enhancing their teaching and their students' learning, and for administrators and teaching developers who are involved in teaching-related decisions on an institutional basis.

Contents

Foreword – Preface – Acknowledgements – Changing university teaching – Constructing learning by aligning teaching: constructive alignment – Formulating and clarifying teaching objectives – Setting the stage for effective teaching – Good teaching: principles and practice – Enriching large class teaching – Teaching international students – Assessing for learning quality I: principles – Assessing for learning quality II: practice – Using educational technology: ET not IT – Some examples of aligned teaching – The reflective teacher – The reflective institution: assuring quality through enhancement – References – Index.

336pp   0 335 21168 2 (Paperback)   0 335 21169 0 (Hardback)

ON BECOMING AN INNOVATIVE UNIVERSITY TEACHER
REFLECTION IN ACTION

John Cowan

This is one of the most interesting texts I have read for many years ... It is authoritative and clearly written. It provides a rich set of examples of teaching, and a reflective discourse.

Professor George Brown

... succeeds in inspiring the reader by making the process of reflective learning interesting and thought provoking ... has a narrative drive which makes it a book too good to put down.

Dr Mary Thorpe

What comes through very strongly and is an admirable feature is so much of the author's own personal experience, what it felt like to take risks and how his own practice developed as a result of taking risks, exploring uncharted territory ... The book has the potential to become the reflective practitioner's "bible".

Dr Lorraine Stefani

This unusual, accessible and significant book begins each chapter by posing a question with which college and university teachers can be expected to identify; and then goes on to answer the question by presenting a series of examples; finally, each chapter closes with "second thoughts", presenting a viewpoint somewhat distinct from that taken by John Cowan. This book will assist university teachers to plan and run innovative activities to enable their students to engage in effective reflective learning; it will help them adapt other teachers' work for use with their own students; and will give them a rationale for the place of reflective teaching and learning in higher education.

Contents

Introduction – What is meant in education by "reflecting"? – What does reflection have to offer in education – Is there a methodology you can and should follow – What can you do to encourage students to reflect? – What is involved for students in analytical reflection? – What is involved in evaluative reflection? – How can you adapt ideas from my teaching, for yours? – How should you get started? – How can such innovations be evaluated? – Where should you read about other work in this field? – A Postscript: final reflections – References – Index – The Society for Research into Higher Education.

192pp   0 335 19993 3 (Paperback)   0 335 19994 1 (Hardback)